# A Walker's Guide to the
# UPPER DERWENT

## By Norman Sanders

Illustrated and designed by Trevor Bolton
Maps drawn by the Author

Whilst every care has been taken by the author and the Peak Park Board in compiling these walks, all the routes described in this book are undertaken at the individual's own risk. Neither the author nor the Peak Park Joint Planning Board can accept any responsibility whatsoever for any consequences arising out of the use of this book, including misinterpretation of the maps and directions.

Published by **Peak Park Joint Planning Board,
Aldern House, Baslow Road,
Bakewell, Derbyshire, DE4 1AE.**

© Norman Sanders, 1984
ISBN 0 907543 85 5

# CONTENTS


**PREFACE** . . . . . . . . . . . . . . . . . . . . . . . . . . . . . . . . . . . . . . . . . . . . . . . . . . . . . . . . 7

**INTRODUCTION**

The area defined. . . . . . . . . . . . . . . . . . . . . . . . . . . . . . . . . . . . . . . . . . . . 10

Geology. . . . . . . . . . . . . . . . . . . . . . . . . . . . . . . . . . . . . . . . . . . . . . . . . . . 10

The importance of wild places. . . . . . . . . . . . . . . . . . . . . . . . . . . . . . . . 12

How to use the book. . . . . . . . . . . . . . . . . . . . . . . . . . . . . . . . . . . . . . . . 12

Visiting the Upper Derwent Valley. . . . . . . . . . . . . . . . . . . . . . . . . . . . . 13

Access Areas in the Peak District National Park. . . . . . . . . . . . . . . . . . 14

Wild life in the area. . . . . . . . . . . . . . . . . . . . . . . . . . . . . . . . . . . . . . . . . 18

The valley before flooding. . . . . . . . . . . . . . . . . . . . . . . . . . . . . . . . . . . 22

The National Trust in the Peak District. . . . . . . . . . . . . . . . . . . . . . . . . 25

The  Maps. . . . . . . . . . . . . . . . . . . . . . . . . . . . . . . . . . . . . . . . . . . . . . . . 26

**THE VALLEYS**

Chapter  1 –  The main Upper Derwent Valley,
Ashopton to the source. . . . . . . . . . . . . . . . . . . . . . . . . . . . . 28

Chapter  2 –  The Upper Derwent Valley,
the side cloughs east of the river. . . . . . . . . . . . . . . . . . . . . 41

Chapter  3 –  The Upper Derwent Valley,
the side cloughs west of the river. . . . . . . . . . . . . . . . . . . . 51

Chapter  4 –  The Westend Valley,
including side cloughs. . . . . . . . . . . . . . . . . . . . . . . . . . . . . . 55

**THE TOPS**

Chapter  5 –  General comments. . . . . . . . . . . . . . . . . . . . . . . . . . . . . . . . 62

Chapter  6 –  Eastern Edges—Derwent Edge  Ashopton to Back Tor. . . . . . . . . . . . . . . . . . 63

Chapter  7 –  Eastern Edges—Howden Edge to Shepherds' Meeting Stones. . . . . . . . . . . . . . . . 67

Chapter  8 –  Ronksley Moor ridge. . . . . . . . . . . . . . . . . . . . . . . . . . . . . . 71

Chapter  9 –  Crook Hill to Alport Castles. . . . . . . . . . . . . . . . . . . . . . . . . 75

Chapter 10 –  Alport Castles to Bleaklow Ridge. . . . . . . . . . . . . . . . . . . . 77

Chapter 11 –  The Alport Valley to Grains in the Water (including ascents from the Snake Road). . 81

Chapter 12 –  Bleaklow Ridge,
Higher Shelf Stones to Barrow Stones. . . . . . . . . . . . . . . . . 85

Chapter 13 –  Suggested walks Nos. 1-15,
Best viewpoints and descents. . . . . . . . . . . . . . . . . . . . . . . 89

**INDEX** . . . . . . . . . . . . . . . . . . . . . . . . . . . . . . . . . . . . . . . . . . . . . . . . . . . . . . . . 94

**LIST OF MAPS** . . . . . . . . . . . . . . . . . . . . . . . . . . . . . . . . . . . . . . . . . . . . . . . . . 97

To my wife—so often a Bleaklow widow but often my companion

and

To the many friendly people I have met on the hills

# PREFACE

Hill and mountains are funny things. To millions they are just another part of the earth's surface, seen fleetingly through a window, and to be avoided. There is no-one there; nothing to do; no money to be made—and they are frightening. To millions more they are impressive objects to be gaped at, and admired, but preferably through a car window and in sunny weather. But over a comparative few, they exert a fascination and love which is difficult to explain and almost impossible to analyse. Is it because in an over-crowded island like ours where all fertile land is cultivated, they alone remain wild and untouched? Is it because of the challenge and the effort needed to get to the tops—a sense of achievement? Is it because they are high up and therefore detached from man? Rhetorical questions—I don't know.

Many of my friends and acquaintances who know that I "walk" treat my modest explorations with tolerant amusement—though they often politely ask where I've been. To them, walking all day, usually alone, over difficult ground in a raging wilderness, possibly in rain or snow, is the act of a lunatic—and perhaps they are right. Much easier, and more sensible, to sit by the fire and watch sport on the telly, or go to the local football match. Yet to those of us who have absorbed this love and fascination, there is nothing like it. The Lakeland North Western fells as you drop down to Keswick on the Dunmail Road, the Howgills glimpsed from the M6, the long, high line of the Pennines—even the lowering humps of Dartmoor—all transmit to us a thrill of excitement and anticipation and a great longing to be among them—to be a minute speck on that distant skyline.

In this book, in addition to suggesting routes up the valleys and on the hills, I have tried to give something of the atmosphere of my homeground—the high moors of North Derbyshire—but whether I have succeeded or not I shall have to leave you to decide.

# THE PEAK NATIONAL PARK
## SHOWING SURROUNDING TOWNS AND THE AREA COVERED BY THE BOOK
**Map 1**

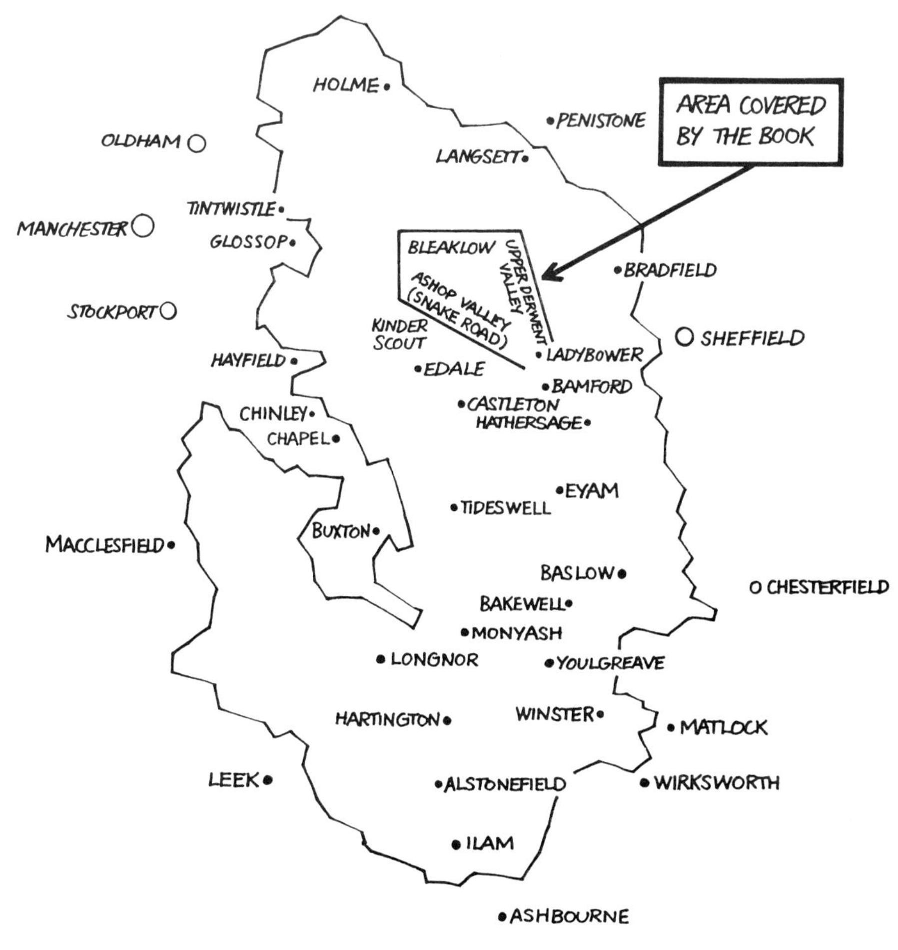

# INTRODUCTION

# INTRODUCTION

# THE AREA DEFINED

This study covers the valley of the Derwent from Ashopton to the source (including the reservoirs), the tributary valleys of the Westend and the Alport, together with the surrounding and intervening high ground, including the Eastern Edges and Bleaklow Ridge. Taking as a base line in the south the A57 main road from Moscar to the Snake Pass summit, the area stretches like a huge irregular horse shoe, going north up Derwent Edge and then right round the water shed to the Snake Pass. To walk that boundary, having once climbed from Ashopton to Derwent Edge, there need be no major descent into a valley. This book includes a look at the past before part of the valley was flooded, comments on hill navigation, birds and mammals to be seen, National Parks and Access, as well as a detailed guide to walks in the valleys and on the hills.

The scenery varies considerably, from the sheer beauty of water and forest in the Derwent Valley to the silent solitude of the high hills. It must be admitted that though these wild moors hold a privileged few in thrall, a great many people, especially city dwellers who are uneasy more than fifty yards from their car, find them intimidating and forbidding. Even so, visitors to the area must be impressed by it, and there are many easy and perfectly safe short walks in lovely surroundings—with just a taste of the wilderness. Locally Derwent Dale surpasses, in my view, the more famous Dovedale or Monsal Dale in grandeur and loveliness, and peaceful spots can more easily be found by the less energetic—without tramping over the heather.

There are may areas of Britain as wild or wilder than Bleaklow but most of them are far from large centres of population. Think of the Highlands of Scotland or Central Wales, for instance. What makes this so remarkable, indeed unique, is that it remains a very real wilderness, yet is surrounded by huge conurbations, housing millions of people. I have often spent an hour lying in the heather at about 2,000 feet, having walked for four hours without seeing anyone, and reflected that only fifteen miles away is the centre of Sheffield. This is, I suppose, why Britain is so odd a country. We are grossly over-populated yet the bulk of the population is crushed into certain areas, leaving the rest of the country largely unspoilt and sparsely populated.

# GEOLOGY (Simplified)

All the rocks in the area are of the Millstone Grit series laid down during the Carboniferous Age of rock building. The sea which then covered most of what is now the north of England, was becoming shallower and great rivers from the north (now Scotland) were washing down vast quantities of sand, grit, mud etc. to fan out and settle on top of the huge thickness of limestone already lying on the sea bed. These substances formed the sandstone, gritstone, shales etc. of today. Layers of loose shale (best example the Edale Shales exposed on Mam Tor, but plenty of others), lay between the various hard strata of gritstone.

The fact that gritstone is so hard, and resists erosion, accounts for the high ground of the area. The remains of the top layer of gritstone—Kinder grit— form the highest points—Barrow Stones—Grinah—Bleaklow Ridge etc. (and Kinder Scout) while the second layer—Middle grit—forms the moorland of Ronksley, Westend Moor, Alport Moor and others—at an almost uniform height.

The valleys cut through these layers are V-shaped and water-formed.

Later, upward earth movements pushed

# THE AREA COVERED BY THE BOOK
## Map 2

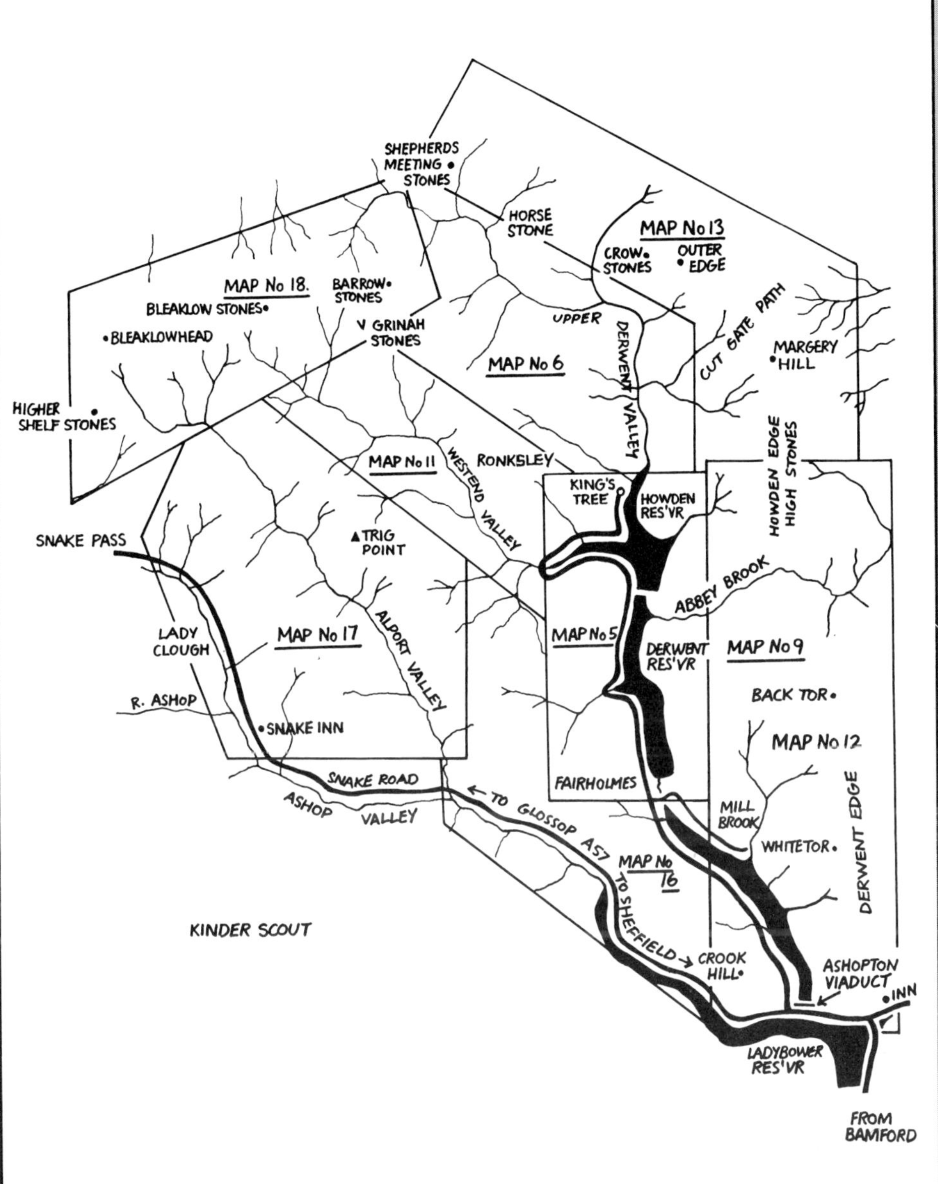

# INTRODUCTION

the rock layers into a dome, so that the strata dipped away to the east and west. The eastward slope can be seen almost anywhere on the Eastern Edges of Howden and Derwent, with the long dip-slope running east to Strines, Bradfield and Flouch. The erosion caused by the river formed the steep scarp slopes up from the Derwent. Since the Mill-stone Grit series is comparatively impervious (unlike the limestone) there is plentiful surface drainage, the rivers themselves often running on bed-rock.

It is interesting to note that the hills up to about 1700 feet were at one time (during warmer climatic conditions), quite heavily forested, as in many places the roots and lower trunks of trees lie under the peat cover and are becoming exposed by erosion. Compared to the rocks, of course, the peat is a very recent covering.

A fascinating feature of the area is the presence of numerous groups of rocks (nearly always named "Stones" but occasionally tors) which appear along the edges. Over the millions of years, these have weathered—mainly by the erosive action of frost and ice—into spectacular shapes. Geographers will be interested to note the instances where the frost has taken advantage of a weakness in the rock, to split it into two. Sometimes the weathering is horizontal, so that the rock appears like a series of wheels, the best example being the aptly named Wheel Stone on Derwent Edge. The walker on the Edges, since he is often above the crag, will tend to miss the rock scenery, and an exploration from below the rock is rewarding—a good example of this situation is Crowstones.

# THE IMPORTANCE OF WILD PLACES – A PERSONAL VIEW

I happen to be one of those people—perhaps I'm growing old or am too pessimistic—who believe that mankind has taken the wrong turning, though (as on a motorway) there is no immediate turning back. The age-old values are dim or forgotten, people seem to want immediate pleasure and are not prepared to search for a more lasting contentment. Noise is preferred to silence and progress is measured by speed and increased gadgetry. To millions, the countryside is something which exists outside their city, to be visited occasionally on warm sunny days, but of which they have no understanding.

Some of the inventions of science, especially in the medical field, must be very gratefully received, but it seems to me we are becoming engulfed in a technological society producing more and more unnecessary luxuries which a gullible and greedy populace has then to be persuaded to consume by unscrupulous advertising. As this machine drives on and on and as the real purpose of living is lost, silence disappears, the night sky is never seen and values rate no higher than the newest colour television. Examples appear everywhere; the people who boast of the huge, expensive meals they have eaten, or tried to eat because it's the thing to do; the persuasive "telly" adverts for costly inessentials, people who cannot work or walk without a transistor set blaring out; and the thousands who seem permanently bored except when being amused.

# INTRODUCTION

But for many it becomes necessary, indeed essential, to get away from all the unreality and tension to a place where mechanical civilisation drops away, and man is left what he really is—a wonderful but insignificant creature facing the elements in a quiet, beautiful, yet untamed setting. And such a setting is the one described in this book.

# VISITING THE UPPER DERWENT VALLEY

Over the past few years, facilities in the Upper Derwent Valley have been improved, both to provide more satisfaction for the many people visiting the area and to ensure that the valley's character is conserved.

A group made up of representatives of major landowners and organisations with a significant interest in the area guides and funds any necessary changes in the valley, along the lines of a joint plan prepared after extensive public consultation.

The car park, toilets, information point, rangers room, cycle hire facilities and new walking routes have all been provided in recent years as part of the plans for the valley. Similarly the road closures and consequent minibus service on Summer Sundays and Bank Holidays.

In 1983 the joint arrangements for this area were "highly commended" in the English Tourist Board's 'Sir Mark Henig Award Scheme' for tourism enterprise. If you have any suggestions as to how facilities at Fairholmes or elsewhere in the valley could be improved, or would like to know more about future plans for the area, please talk to the local Ranger or the assistant at the Information Point.

*Derwent Dam*

# INTRODUCTION

# ACCESS AREAS IN THE PEAK DISTRICT NATIONAL PARK

The Peak District became Britain's first National Park in 1951. Before that time much of its open moorland was forbidden territory to walkers, who were kept off by gamekeepers (who were instructed to protect the landowners' grouse from disturbance) and the Water Boards' bailiffs (who were anxious to maintain the purity of the waters running into the reservoirs supplying nearby cities with drinking water).

Pressure for the "freedom to roam" over areas such as Kinder Scout and Bleaklow was one of the factors that led up to the formation of the National Parks of England and Wales. Fears over grouse disturbance proved to be unfounded, and new filter plants made the strict protection of the water gathering grounds unnecessary. Within a few years of the designation of the Peak District as a National Park, agreements were reached between the Park and landowners permitting free access to walkers over some moors for all but a few days each year when grouse shooting is taking place, or access is withdrawn because of a fire risk or other emergency.

The formation of the country's first Ranger Service (then called Wardens) stemmed from the need to patrol these newly negotiated Access Areas, particularly on the twelve or so days between 12th August and 10th December when grouse shooting was taking place.

Now there are nearly 80 square miles of Access Areas in the Peak District National Park, covering nearly 15% of the Park's 542 square mile area.

As in most of this country's National Parks, most of the land within the Peak District boundaries remains privately owned. This is why walkers should keep to the public footpaths, except in Access Areas and on National Trust land. Rangers will be found in all parts of the National Park, advising visitors, liaising with farmers and landowners, and giving practical help in resource management and emergencies.

Visitors making use of the Access Areas are required to observe a commonsense set of bye-laws, including keeping dogs on a lead at all times and not lighting fires. Permission to camp on these areas can only be given by the individual owners of access moors, and is rarely granted, but there are a number of excellent camping sites adjacent to these Access Areas.

# INTRODUCTION

# NAVIGATION AND SURVIVAL ON THE HILLS

Many thousands of words have been written on this subject and much advice given—some of it good and some of it stupid. One of the most stupid things suggested is that when caught in the mist, you should remain where you are and wait for help to arrive. How the devil can you stay put at 2,000 feet with the temperature below zero and only two hours of daylight left? Even if you took the right action, got out of the wind and so on, you'd probably be dead long before help arrived. Yet this advice is sometimes still given. In open country, such as the Bleaklow area, except in the case of injury (this is a different thing entirely) there should be no difficulty in descending to a valley, and thence to some sort of civilisation, though the walk may be long. The thing to remember is that once you have reached lower ground, and have proceeded downstream to (say) the forests of the Upper Derwent or the Westend, survival is almost certain, whereas at Bleaklow Stones, death is almost certain during many months of the year.

I have noticed that even amongst quite experienced walkers, the Bleaklow Moors are viewed with some awe as being a highly dangerous area. Listening sometimes, I have wondered whether they were talking about North Derbyshire or the Himalayas. The truth is that Bleaklow is both more and less dangerous than its reputation. That sounds daft so I'll try to explain. It is more dangerous because it is, for England, a large, almost featureless area, much of it above 1500 feet, with a maze of gullies (cloughs) and small valleys. Many of the valleys in mist and poor visibility look the same, as do many of the ridges, unless you know them well. Thus, with the cloud down to perhaps 1100 feet

the whole area is wrapped in gloom and damp cotton wool. In this sort of situation the walker who doesn't know where he is, and who hasn't studied the lie of the land, may choose to walk by compass in a direction which necessitates nine or ten miles of very rough walking before a road is reached, and the walker will be likely to be exhausted or in darkness, or both, before that. In winter or in severe conditions, this would be very serious, and probably fatal. Now—and this is why it is less dangerous—had the walker 'known where he was, and had he previously (but on the spot if necessary) studied the map, there is nowhere on Bleaklow where the safety of a valley cannot be reached by compass walking within two miles—and usually much less. May I give one example. Imagine, say, two walkers having left their car at the King's Tree for a circular walk, finishing down Ronksley, being caught by descending cloud which reduces visibility to ten yards, a little way west of Bleaklow Stones. It is early December, the time two o'clock in the afternoon and it is beginning to sleet. They are experienced enough not to panic (the likely reaction, and one that is nearly always disastrous) but not at all sure where they are, and they soon lose all real sense of direction. Since they were walking generally east, they decide to continue by compass in that direction. After an hour or so rough walking, under increasing difficulties, they would descend to the Derwent Valley, but if the cloud was by this time at valley level, they might not recognise it and so push on. Ahead would be mile upon mile of appalling ground, with no possibility of reaching a road before dark. Growing cold and weariness would almost certainly lead to disaster. Now, if the walkers had known exactly where they were and had been aware of the lie of the valleys, having assessed the rapidly deteriorating weather conditions, they would run for safety; by turning and walking by compass south-east, they would be descending within

# INTRODUCTION

minutes, and would have reached the safety of the Westend Valley within half an hour, leaving themselves a straight-forward walk on path and track back to the Westend gate—then by road to the car.

Detailed knowledge of these hills and the smaller cloughs and gullies can be only obtained by repeated visits and exploration, but the general direction of the ridges and main valleys can be learnt in five minutes by studying an O.S. 1:25000 map and this is enough to keep out of trouble. Let me tabulate it:

1. The main Bleaklow Ridge—Higher Shelf, Wain Stones, Bleaklow Stones, Barrow Stones—runs almost west-east, and parallel to this, a couple of miles or less to the north, is the Etherow Valley.

2. The Eastern Edges—Outer Edge, Howden Edge, Back Tor, Derwent Edge—run roughly north-south, and parallel to them a mile or so to the west is the Derwent Valley.

3. The three main tributaries of the Derwent—the Westend, Alport and Ashopton (with Lady Clough) run roughly north-west to south-east with ridges in between the valleys.

Thus, the area can be represented in diagrammatic form—see Map No. 3.

There will be many variations depending on where you are aiming for, but the basic rules will, I hope, be clear.

(a) Anywhere on the Bleaklow Ridge with the objective in the Etherow Valley, steer north.

(b) Almost anywhere on the Bleaklow Ridge with the objective—or safety—in the tributary valleys, steer south. The only variation here would be at the western edge in the vicinity of Higher Shelf Stones, where the safe way off would be Crooked Clough or the Pennine Way to the head of the Snake Pass.

(c) Anywhere on the Eastern Edges, steer west for the Derwent Valley or east for Ewden, Flouch etc.

There are two main areas where the headwaters of two river systems almost run into one another, so that great care is needed in mist. The first is the area just west of Bleaklow Stones where the headwater gullies of the Alport and the Westend are only yards apart and indeed in one place almost join. Do not, therefore, in descending from Bleaklow Stones, assume that the first gullies you meet are those for which you are looking. If your car is on the Snake Road, and you turn down the Westend instead of the Alport (for Grains-in-the-Water) you'll be going away from your car. Check carefully with the compass. (If your car is by the Westend forest gate and you erroneously follow the Alport Valley, the mistake is not so serious—you can always return to your starting point via Alport Castles.)

A more serious mistake can occur in the area north-east of Bleaklow Stones where the headwaters of the Derwent and Far Black Clough almost intermingle. This is a peaty featureless section of groughs and gullies, and in thick mist only a careful check on the compass can ensure you are on course. A mistake here would also be more serious, since you would finish up in the Etherow Valley to the north, instead of the King's Tree—to the south—(or vice versa) a long, long way apart.

One last word; walking in thick mist by a compass bearing is never as easy as it sounds in the guide books. The eerie closed-in atmosphere makes fear creep closer and panic easy. A quite well-known mile to, say, a valley, seems never-ending and you become convinced you are going wrong, so time yourself—a mile will need half an hour, perhaps more. Never "think you know the way". I have several times gone quite seriously wrong through being too clever and walking on my supposed knowledge of the ground and vegetation

# GENERAL DIRECTIONS FOR NAVIGATION
## TO GET OUT OF TROUBLE
**Map 3**

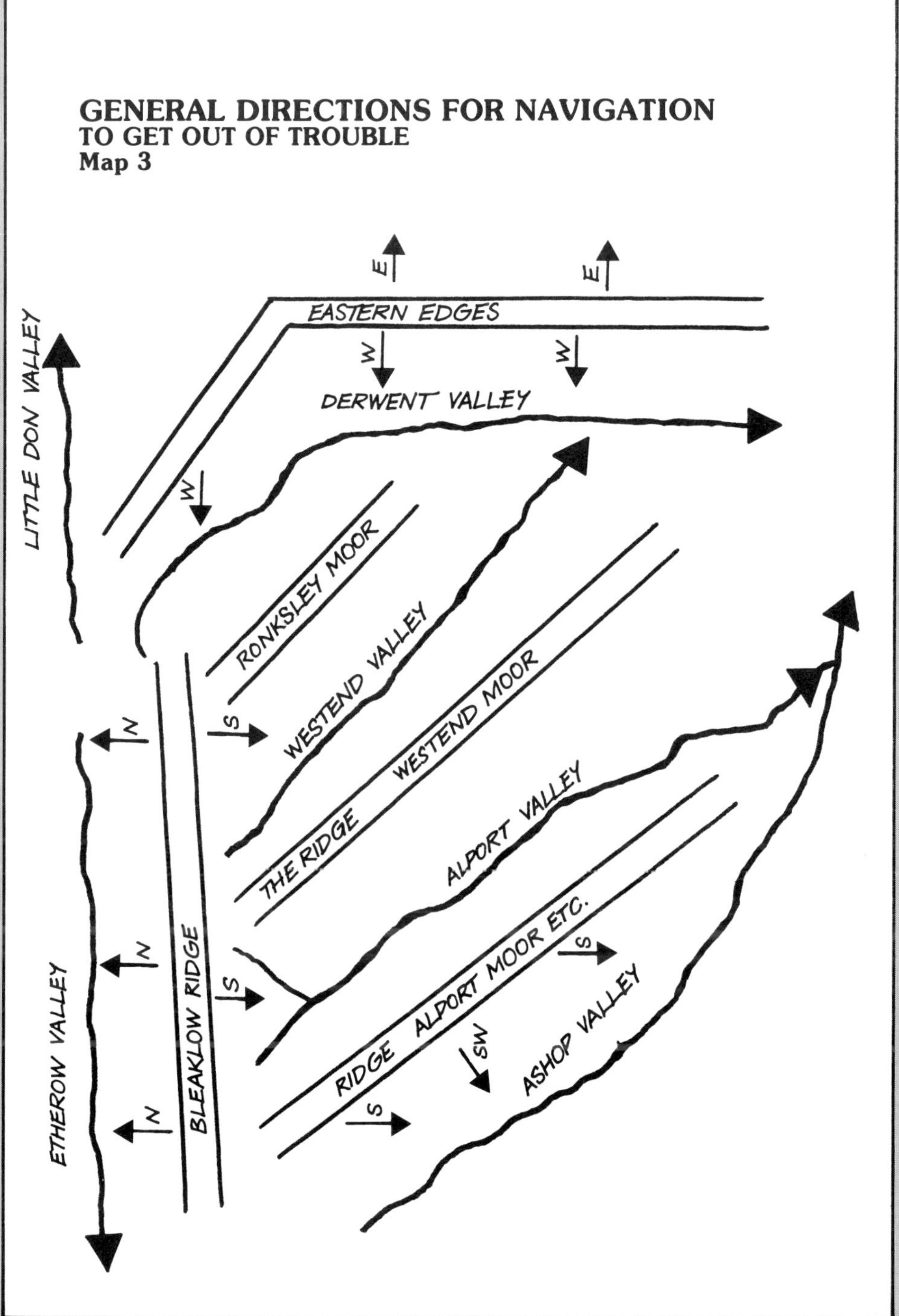

# INTRODUCTION

(though this can help enormously) ignoring the compass; and once you have blundered, you don't know where you are, making further progress difficult. So keep calm, a valley is near, and trust the compass.

## WILDLIFE IN THE AREA

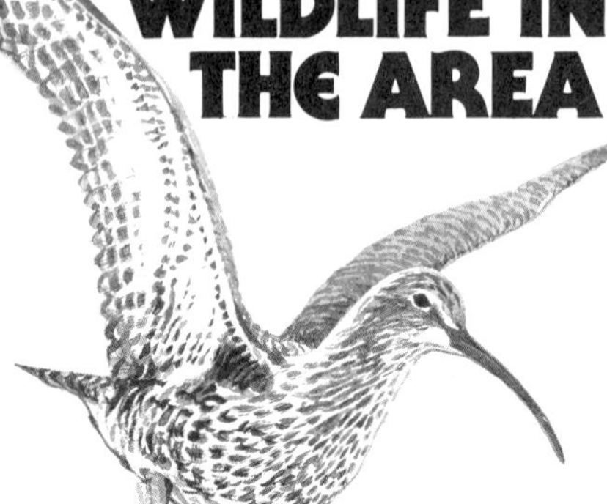


No-one can wander in the valleys and over the hills without becoming interested in the birds and animals. The reservoirs themselves do not support any large population of water birds, mainly because, I am told, the banks dip so steeply that a few feet out, the water is deep. Thus there are few marshy shallows beloved by geese etc. Nevertheless, duck and occasionally geese are in evidence, and even—if you are lucky—a few goldeneye. I always particularly enjoy the duck calling as the light fades near Grainfoot, where I have on occasion counted twelve Mallard. I have also on rare occasions seen a heron, but you have to be fortunate—and quiet.

In the often dense forest and undergrowth round most of the water, there is the usual resident population of blackbirds, thrushes, robins etc.—more numerous south of about the Howden Dam. This population is reinforced by warblers and other small birds in the spring and summer and there always seems to be a number of cuckoos. I have often heard my first cuckoo, not in the woods further south but high up in the Derwent Valley but why the bird should fly over so much lush country to so remote and inhospitable a spot goodness knows. Crossbills can also be seen in and around the forests, with dippers and wagtails on the Derwent itself.

On the moors, the population is more specialised. Throughout the winter, the only resident is the incredibly hardy red grouse. They become more gregarious at this time, and it is always interesting on the first warmer day of late winter to hear them becoming vocal, cackling and clucking away to themselves of their females. Their famous "go-back" call is well known, but they also make a series of odd noises which can, from a distance, be mistaken for human conversation. Their eggs are laid in a hollow, with virtually no nest, and, when approached, the bird leaves them only at the last second. It is disconcerting to have the silence shattered by the female's harsh raucous voice, a split second before the boot descends near the nest. Later it is always fascinating—no matter how many times you have seen it before to witness the "broken wing" technique as the adult bird limps over the heather, luring the intruder away from the young birds.

In spring the high places really come to life. Skylarks, pipits, and in rocky places, wheatears populate the slopes and of course on the boggy tops are the waders. Curlew—whose haunting call is a yearly joy—golden plover, redshank, dunlin and snipe can all be found, especially on the flatter and wetter tops. The golden plover in particular is noticeable, calling repeatedly from the ground, and has an endearing habit of escorting the walker off his (or her) territory. It is one of the significant and anticipatory points of the year when the sad piping of the first plover is heard— sometimes as early as February. Kestrels are also fairly common anywhere in the area.

# INTRODUCTION

The odd visitor or migrant blown off course, can also appear. I once saw what was almost certainly a snow bunting in wintry conditions near Hoar Clough, and one late afternoon a barn owl glided across the hillside below me as I sat at Grinah.

The only large mammal resident and regularly seen on or near the tops apart from sheep, is the white (or mountain) hare. These are always a delight to see, especially in spring when, if you are lucky, you may see their strange ritual when, I am told, the males compete for dominance. Their white colour, though excellent camouflage in snow, makes them stand out in ordinary conditions, and it changes to a buff colour, like that of ordinary hares, in late spring. Shepherds

and the keeper tell me there are foxes on the hills—and indeed I have seen their droppings—but only once have I seen one high up—near the source of the Derwent. I have, however, seen them in or near the forests at lower levels. Red squirrels used to inhabit the forests also, but the last I saw was several years ago, so I think they may have been almost driven out by the fairly numerous grey variety. These, I have no doubt, do damage, but are nevertheless a delight to watch. If you surprise one in an isolated fairly small tree it is amusing to see it edge round the trunk to keep itself "invisible" as you walk round, so that only the tiny paws can be seen, changing position. I have twice seen weasels up in the hills—once near the foot of Barrow Clough, and once near Horse Stone. They were both extremely inquisitive and spent about ten minutes peering at me from vantage points in the heather at a distance of about six feet. On both occasions it was summer, and I imagine they retreat down the valley as winter approaches.

Small lizards can be seen, especially on the south-facing slopes of the Eastern Edges during warm weather in late spring or summer. They are very fast and shoot quickly into thick heather for safety. I have never seen a snake of any type, but there are some in the area.

# INTRODUCTION

No-one, of course, can walk on these moors without being aware of the hill sheep. Unlike their pampered brethren of the lowlands, these are, by and large, left to fend for themselves, often in appalling conditions. In a harsh winter, it is pathetic to see them pawing the snow to scrape down a bit of dried, coarse grass. Yet in the main they survive, and often look amazingly fit as winter reluctantly ends. In my observation, the losses mainly occur in deep drifted snow, where the animals have taken shelter in a gully or hollow and have been thickly covered over. Their bodies can be seen singly or a few huddled together as the snow melts—a sad sight. Visitors not used to the area will probably be surprised that there are comparatively so few sheep to such a large area of hill country. They must reflect that the grazing is so poor that many acres are required to support even one sheep. I don't think even their most ardent admirers would claim any great intelligence for sheep, yet it is surprising how they can learn. Kinder sheep, for example, see so many people that they are almost tame. Some of them will take the sandwich out of the box if you're not looking. Bleaklow sheep, seeing so few, remain wild and run panic-stricken when surprised. But I have noticed, especially round the King's Tree, they now congregate round the cars, and visitors— flattered perhaps—feed them. This is not a good thing—motorists please note.

One of the dangers at lambing time is that of the small lambs falling into peat-holes. Any walker on these hills will know that there are many of these holes, often obscured by reeds or heather, which constitute a danger especially in snow— and they are also a danger to the lambs. I have on four occasions rescued one— being alerted by the plaintive cries issuing from the earth. In three cases, having hauled up the lamb from the peaty depths (no easy task) and warmed it up, it was impossible to locate the mother. No doubt she had given up hope and wandered off— but this necessitated carrying the lamb miles back to the car and then to the appropriate farmer. It is amusing how quickly you become "mother" to the lamb, which soon seeks your warmth and comfort. I once found a fully grown sheep three-quarters submerged in a peat pool and had to spend an unpleasant half-hour—assisted by my wife—pulling it out; and the sheep didn't help at all. *

*But please remember—a ewe often leaves a lamb while she grazes, so providing the lamb is in a safe place you should normally leave it alone.*

*White-faced Woodland tups*

*Swaledale ewe with her lamb*

Many people these days have either been to a sheep-dog trial or seen it on the television, and I too enjoy those—but there are few better hill-sights than that of the shepherd gathering across a hillside. The masterly handling of the dogs, the intelligence of the dogs themselves, and the speed at which this apparently gigantic operation is carried through, is superb. The other thing I like, if you are caught in the middle of the gathering and pause to watch, is the way the dogs completly ignore your presence. They have a job to do and are not to be distracted by stupid walkers.

I hope I have made it clear in these notes that there are lots of living things to be seen on these apparently lifeless hills. One last thing, if you take a dog with you anywhere in the area, make sure it is under absolute control, and on a lead on all access or National Trust land. And don't forget this does not apply just at lambing time in April—the sheep are carrying lambs through January, February and March and great damage can be done by rampaging dogs.

*Derbyshire
Gritstone Sheep*

# THE VALLEY BEFORE FLOODING

I suppose no-one now is alive who can remember the whole valley before flooding (though many—including myself—can remember the Derwent-Ashopton section before the Ladybower was built). Not only was there no reservoir water, but there were no forests, so the valley must have been very different. Whether it was more or less beautiful is a moot point—academic—and depends on taste.

The map included here (Map no. 4) is based on an old Ordnance Survey sheet dated around the turn of the century, which was given to me in my local pub many years ago. One thing always strikes me when I look at it, is the number of farms which existed. The valley was narrow at or above 800 feet, and there couldn't have been very much fertile land. Yet—if my count is correct—there were fourteen farms north of Derwent. What a silent, detached existence it must have been in this remote dead-end valley at the turn of the century. About six miles for the farmer at Westend Farm to have a drink in the bright lights and wild gaiety of the nearest pub in Ashopton and then six miles back—perhaps the horse would know the way.

Several of the farms above the water line north of the Derwent dam—Marebottom, Lockerbrook and Gores—still exist, but with all the best land gone so that they were no longer viable working units, they are used for other purposes. Several other farms higher up the valley were also above the waterline Ridge, Banktop and Westend—but presumably they were too remote for use to be made of them. I have failed even to find the site of Westend Farm, though it's possible to locate where it must have stood near the bottom of Fagney Clough. Presumably the later forestry workings have obliterated all trace. The site of Ridge Farm, with a few stones lying about, can be found on the path up through Ridge Wood, near the edge of the forest, but the one still standing (though a ruin and crumbling away more and more each year) is Banktop. Here one can imagine what it must have been like to live there, looking down on the Westend Valley. But, if you have imagination, the atmosphere is very strange. Whenever I approach it from Ridge Clough, especially on a still, dull day, I have an odd feeling of apprehension—almost fear. I imagine what life must have been like—people talking and shouting, hating and loving, hoping

# DERWENT DALE (ASHOPTON TO HOWDEN) BEFORE FLOODING

**Map 4**

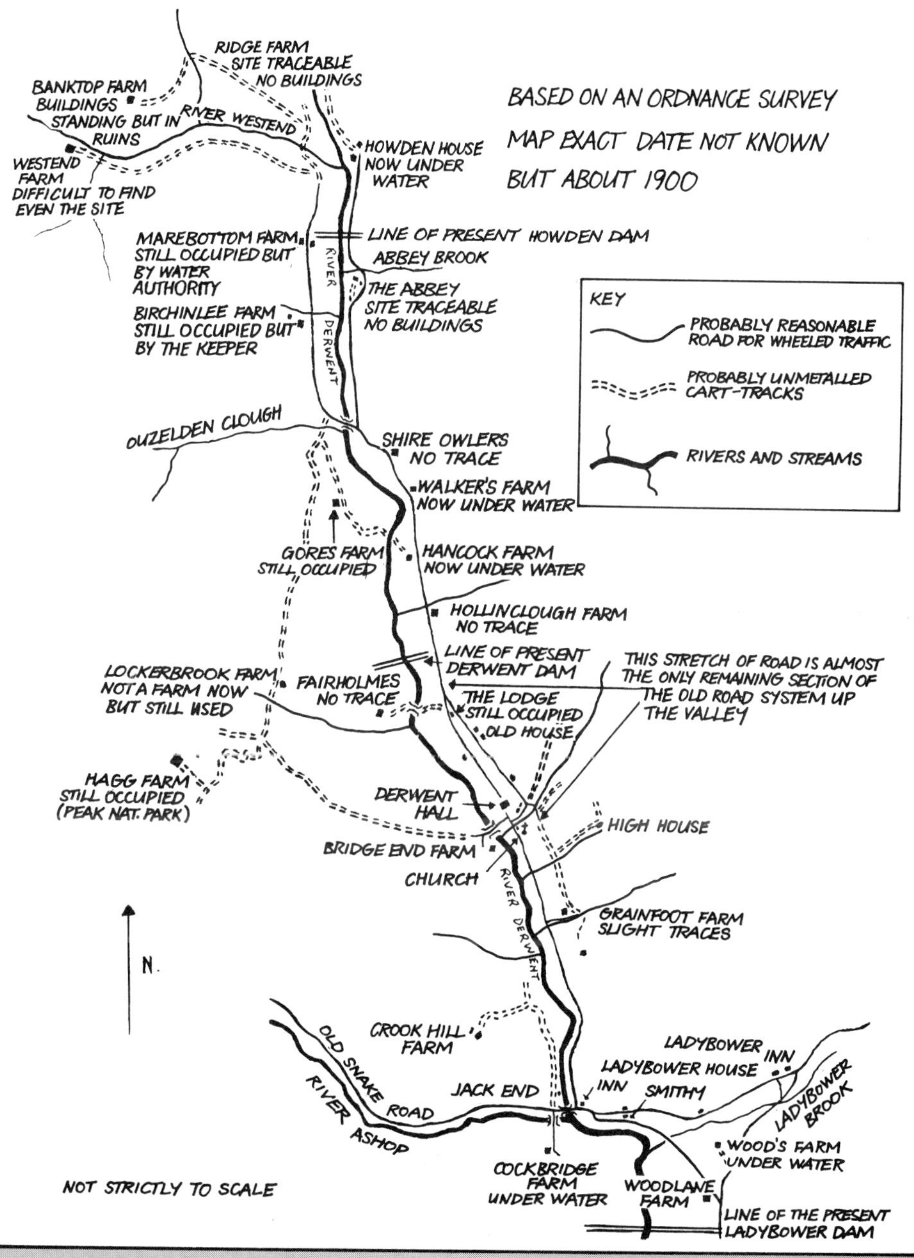

# INTRODUCTION

*Ashopton*

desperately for good markets, desolated by poor ones. And now it is all long since over, with the house utterly still and deserted. I steal thankfully away along the forest edge.

South of the Derwent Dam, the valley was, of course, flooded by the opening of the Ladybower Reservoir—much later in 1945/6. Most of the hamlets of Derwent—with its Hall, Church and packhorse bridge (rebuilt at Slippery Stones)—and Ashopton, with its inn and smithy—are under water. Mr. Ollerenshaw's old farm at Derwent, and Mr. Elliott's at Ashopton happily survive but most of the others, both in the Derwent and Ashop valleys, have gone. The 2½ inch O.S. map shows

Grainfoot farm as still existing, but it doesn't, though the site can be traced.

Whether you regret the passing of the farms and hamlets or not, you can only be thankful for the beauty that remains. As I walked back along the Reservoir track some weeks ago to my car near the Derwent Dam, I was thinking these sort of thoughts. It was a completely still January day with thin sunshine. The water on both reservoirs was like a mirror, reflecting perfectly the hills and forest on the other side. There was only the odd water sound—and it was all magnificent—so perhaps we should be thankful to the old Water Authorities.

# INTRODUCTION

## THE NATIONAL TRUST IN THE PEAK DISTRICT

The National Trust and the National Park, whilst separate and different organisations, work together towards similar aims in the Peak District. The Trust, a charitable organisation relying for its funds primarily on donations and its members' subscriptions, does in fact own about 12% of the land in the National Park, nearly all of it open to free public access.

Its holdings include much of the moorland described in this walking guide, and some 30,000 acres in and around this area are managed by National Trust Wardens as part of the Trust's High Peak Estate. At the time of writing (1983) the National Trust has acquired, with the help of a large loan, 3,000 acres of Kinder Scout's wild moorland plateau together with some adjacent farmland. The Trust is urgently appealing to the public for £200,000 to pay off this loan and secure the future of this unique area. Donations should be sent to: P.O. Box 1, Ashbourne, Derbyshire.

## HOW TO USE THIS BOOK

Some people visiting the Upper Derwent Valley will want to do no more than admire the scenery from the valley; some will enjoy short and easy walks; and some will wish to explore the tops and more remote spots. I have, therefore, largely divided the book into three parts:

(a) **The valleys – the Derwent, Westend and Alport (Chapters 1 and 4).**

(b) **The main side cloughs – which can be used either as an extension of an easy valley walk or as an access route to the ridges (Chapters 2 and 3).**

(c) **The tops themselves (Chapters 5-12).**

Thus a family on a four or five mile walk from the King's Tree could use the "King's Tree to the source" chapter up the valley track, and then the section of Broadhead Clough for further exploration. The walker out for the day could use the same sections but as a route to the Eastern Edges at Crow Stones—thence using the appropriate chapter of "The Tops"; and similarly up the Westend or Abbey Brook. That's the idea anyway—I hope it works. I have also given short summaries of circular walks at the back of the book. These are cross-referred to the maps and text.

# INTRODUCTION

# THE MAPS

Before the signing of the Access Agreements, the entire area covered by this study was pathless, with the exception of a very few public footpaths and the shooters' paths. Almost all paths shown on the maps, therefore, have been made by the feet of walkers since that time. Most walkers tend to select the easiest route over rough ground so that where the direction is obvious, clear paths have evolved but these are by no means continuous, since the clearness of a path often depends on the type of ground over which it passes. Thus, through low heather, a path is quite quickly made, but if the route further on passes across half a mile of peat groughs and bog, no path is produced because walkers chose slightly different lines to traverse the awkward ground. A further fact is, of course, the number of people who use the route. Readers should, therefore, note when planning a walk that whereas the route may start off clearly it may deteriorate into a pathless waste in a couple of miles. Furthermore, in the circumstances outlined, the paths will not be entirely static. On a route for which I have indicated no path, one may have developed by the time you read this.

How to indicate some of the tracks also caused a certain amount of difficulty. For example, would it be correct to use the same symbol for the track up the east side of the reservoirs which, though private, could easily be used by a car, as for the rough route running up the Abbey Brook valley—which definitely couldn't be used by an ordinary car? Yet the latter for much of its length is definitely not a narrow footpath. In the end, I decided that if the route was wide, say approximately the width of a car, and with a reasonably level surface, it would be shown as a track, but readers should note there will be variations.

I have tried to keep the maps as simple as possible. Initially, I drew them showing a number of contour lines, but subsequently decided that these tended to confuse the issue. I have, therefore, included only a few significant contours, and these only to indicate a ridge, but a number of spot heights have been shown. In any case, the maps are meant to be used in conjunction with the excellent Ordnance Survey maps which are available. In particular, the O.S. Dark Peak outdoor leisure map at 1:25,000 scale is invaluable for walking this area, showing rights of way and their status, they can be bought from National Park Information Centres (at Edale, Castleton and Bakewell) or good bookshops.

The larger scale sketches, included to show the details of some particular areas, are—as indicated thereon—not strictly to scale.

**THE KEY TO THE MAPS IS AS FOLLOWS:**

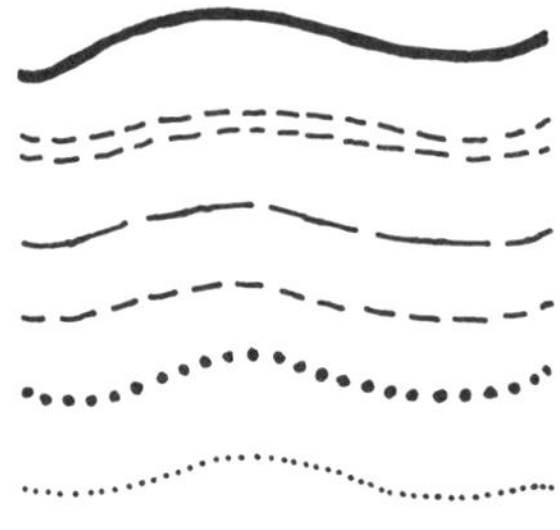

*Motor roads*

*Tracks or a wide path, but usually quite unsuitable for vehicles*

*A clear distinct path*

*A faint and/or intermittent path*

*No path but a reasonable route, though often rough going.*

*Contour lines*

# THE VALLEYS

# THE MAIN UPPER DERWENT VALLEY

# ASHOPTON TO THE SOURCE

Derwent Dale is the central valley of this study. From Ashopton to just north of the King's Tree (where the road ends) the valley is, of course, flooded by the arm of the Ladybower Reservoir and the Derwent and Howden Reservoirs. On the west side, a motor road runs alongside the water all the way to the King's Tree roundabout, from which point the motorist must needs return. This road is rather narrow and to avoid the congestion which has occurred in the past, it is closed on summer Sundays and Bank Holidays from Fairholmes northwards. The road below the Derwent Dam to Mill Brook is closed to all motor vehicles at all times (except for local access). There are a few exemptions to the Derwent Lane closure for those requiring access to property, and for the essential public services—Police, Ambulance and Fire Brigade. Cars displaying a disabled person's orange badge or disc are also allowed through. A mini-bus service provides access (on those days when Derwent Lane is closed), from the car park and picnic area at Fairholmes, or you can hire bikes from the Cycle Hire Centre. Full details are given in leaflets available at Fairholmes.

No directional guidance is needed on such a clear route, but the road itself is of some interest. Before the flooding of the dale, the road to Derwent village and the isolated farms ran up the valley bottom. If you are interested in what the valley was like before flooding, see the section in the Introduction and the sketch map showing the old tracks and farms based on a pre-1900 O.S. map.

HOWDEN DAM

# DERWENT VALLEY RESERVOIR SECTION
## DERWENT TO THE KING'S TREE
### Map 5

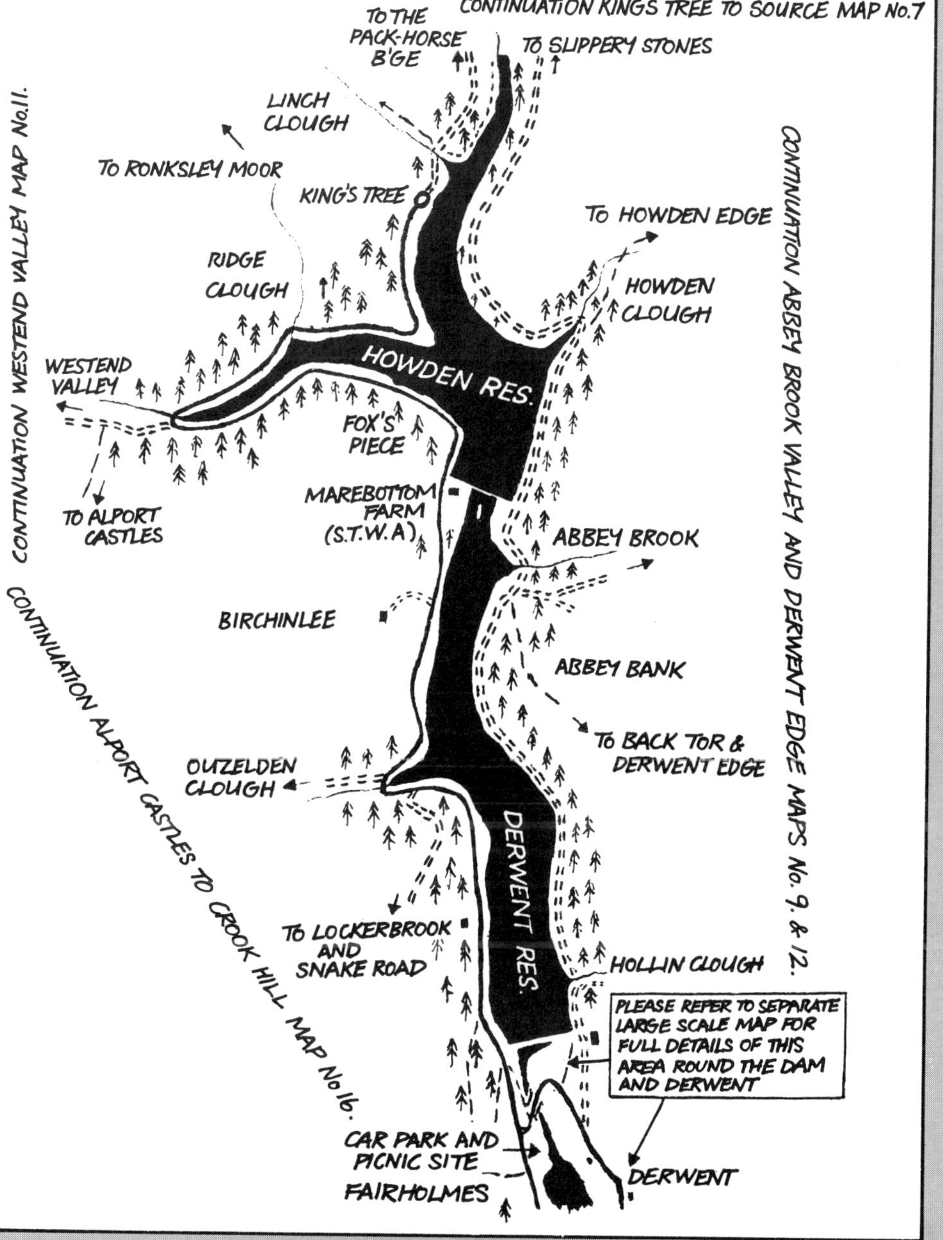

# THE VALLEYS
## The main Upper Derwent Valley, Ashopton to the source

### A BRIEF COMMENT ON THE HISTORY OF THE RESERVOIRS

Before the construction of the Howden and Derwent Dams, a railway was built from the main line near Bamford Station to a point just short of the Howden Dam, for the conveyance of the gritstone blocks (from the quarry near Grindleford) and other material. A temporary village, popularly known as Tin Town, was built just below Birchinlee to house the workmen and their families. Traces of this can still be seen amongst the trees.

When the Howden Dam was finished, the railway lines were pulled up, but traces of the route can still be seen — piles in the reservoir bank at the entrance of Ouzelden Clough when the water level is low; an old bridge near Fairholmes; and at various points in the forests alongside the reservoirs.

The Derwent Reservoir and Dam were used as a practice ground for the famous "bouncing bomb", which was to be so effectively used against similar dams in the Ruhr Valley during the Second World War. The Dam Busters film was also made in the Upper Derwent Valley.

South of the Derwent Dam, the road followed the river in the bottom of the valley, through Derwent village, until that part too was submerged by the rising waters of the Ladybower Reservoir in the mid-forties. I can remember cycling up that road to stay at Derwent Hall when it was a Youth Hostel in the late thirties, and a lovely road it was. When this last flooding took place, the present road was constructed on the west side of the water, leaving a track on the east bank.

# THE AREA AROUND THE DERWENT DAM
## Map 6

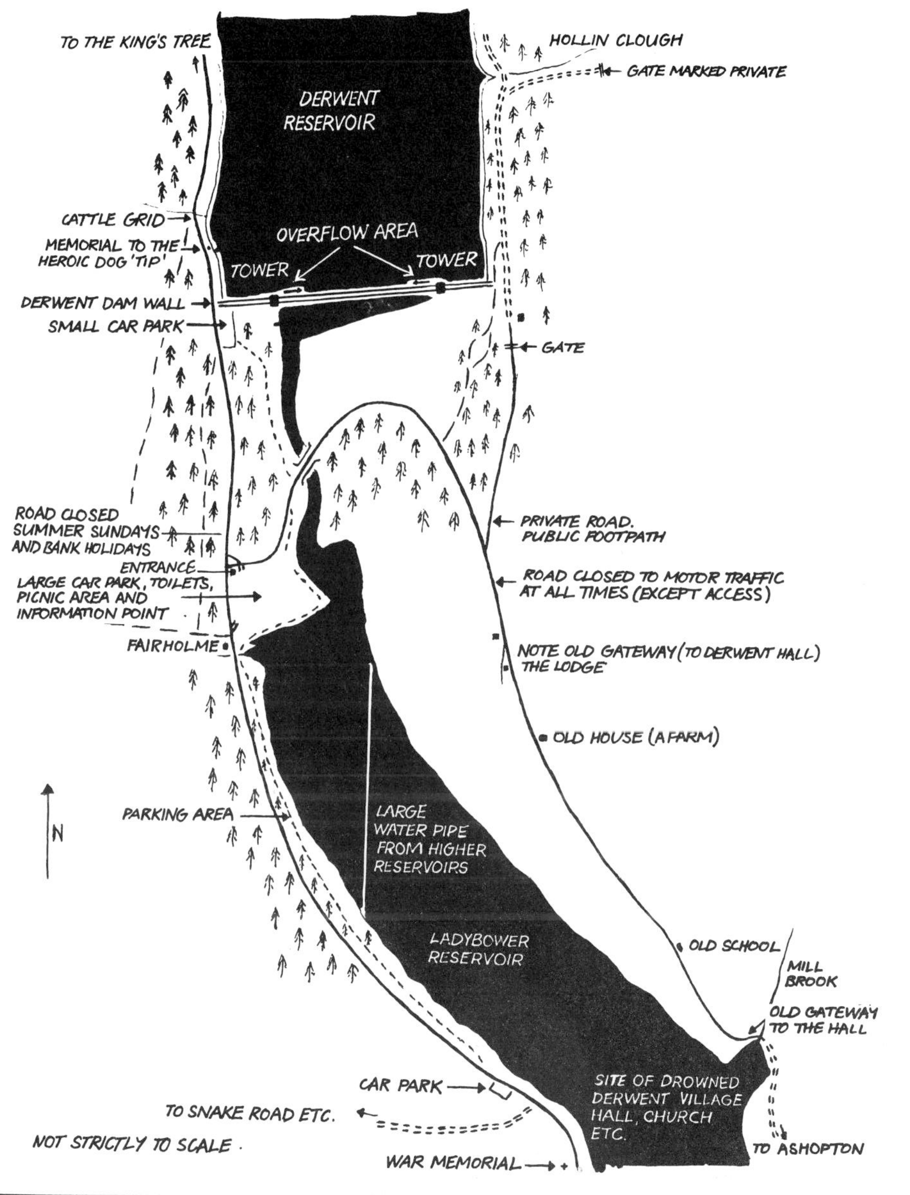

# THE VALLEYS
## The main Upper Derwent Valley, Ashopton to the source

### THE WEST BANK OF THE RESERVOIRS

Although this book is mainly concerned with walking routes on rights-of-way and Access/National Trust land, it must be said that even from a car window the road from the Ashopton Viaduct northwards to the King's Tree is scenically superb by any comparison, and well worth a visit. In some lights, on sparkling blue mornings in early summer, or on still, shining evenings, the hills and trees and water combine to produce scenes of exceptional beauty, which compare well with the Lake District or the lochs of north-west Scotland. It is, in my view, the only part of the Peak District which can equal the beauty and serenity of, say, Buttermere or Ullswater.

The road turns northwards off the Snake Road, at the western end of the Ashopton Viaduct, and climbs gently across the hillside. The views are immediately excellent across the water to the forested and bracken-covered slopes of Lead Hill. Just short of Hurst Clough (a blaze of colour in autumn) there is a useful parking space to the east of the road, which is also a pleasant view point. From here, and from the next mile or so of road, most of Derwent Edge can be traced on the skyline, with (from south to north) Wheel Stones, White Tor, Dovestone Tor and further round, the pimple of Lost Lad clearly visible. Just before a curve in the road, and above what was Derwent village, is the War Memorial to the men from the village who were killed. It is sad to think of them leaving such a quiet and peaceful spot to be slaughtered in horror on a foreign battlefield.

At Fairholmes there are excellent parking, toilet and picnic facilities, as well as an information point open summer Sundays and Bank Holidays and a Cycle Hire centre. The site has been tastefully constructed amidst the trees, and will, I think, develop as the principal venue in the Dale. It is a good starting point for long walks to Back Tor, Abbey Brook, Alport Castles, and others and also for many short strolls around the dam wall or along the road to Mill Brook. Suggested walks Nos. 4, 5, 6, 7 and 8 start here.

The road climbs to the western end of the Derwent Dam (have a look at the water pouring in from the tunnel) and just beyond is the memorial to the dog "Tip", famous for his fidelity to his dead master on the Howden Moors. The story is told briefly on the tablet—interesting that the dog managed to stay alive, whereas the man died—are dogs tougher than humans?

There are lovely views over the water, as the road proceeds northwards, past Gore's Farm and round the inlet of Ouzelden Clough. In Birchinlee West Plantation are the remains of the temporary village built when the dams were under construction, and higher up the hillside, Birchinlee House. Excellent views again here to the east, through the trees and up the long valley of Abbey Brook to the Eastern Edges.

Just after Marebottom Farm (a farm no longer) the road climbs to the end of the Howden Dam wall, and from the corner is a lovely prospect across the water and towards the head of the reservoir. The road now goes down the long arm of the Westend inlet and back up the other side— infuriating to tired walkers who must slog nearly two miles to gain a three hundred yards advance. At the King's Tree (or Royal Oak) the road ends in a roundabout, where limited parking is available during weekdays, and further progress must be on foot.

After Fairholmes (the main starting point for walks—see leaflet), King's Tree is the start for a number of walks—long and short—in the upper valley. There are no problems as a clear track, used by the Forestry Authority officials, Water staff and shepherds, leads north over the stepping stones at the foot of Linch Clough. From here the easy way is simply to continue on

# DERWENT VALLEY
## KING'S TREE TO THE SOURCE INCLUDING RONKSLEY MOOR
### Map 7

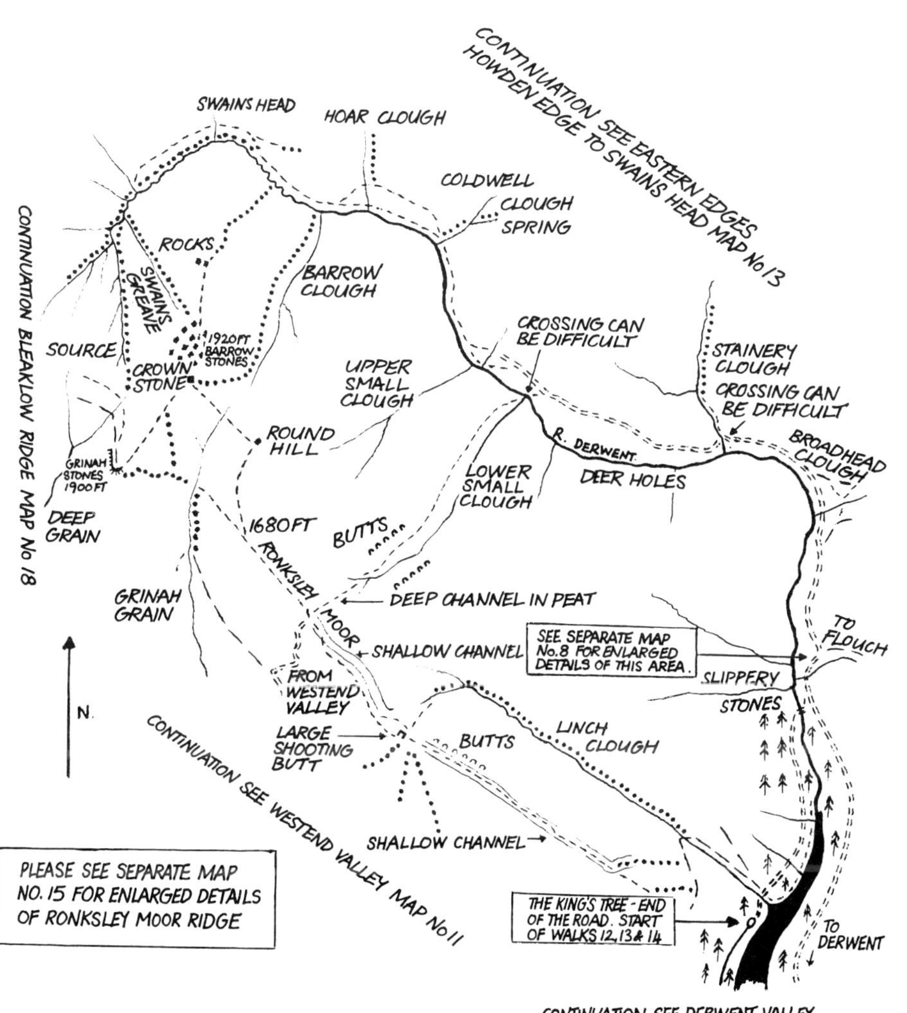

# THE VALLEYS
## The main Upper Derwent Valley, Ashopton to the source

the track through the forest for half a mile until it ends and a path goes down to the Packhorse Bridge. There is a waterworks track going off to the river just before this, giving access for their vehicles. An alternative to the track is to turn right along the water's edge after the Linch Clough stream and follow a rough path to the actual end of the reservoir, thence through the forest by the edge of the river. This route is interesting and the views good.

## THE EAST BANK OF THE RESERVOIRS

The track on the east side of the reservoirs is always a delight. It runs a long way—from the Ashopton Viaduct to Slippery Stones—and except for a stretch from the Mill Brook inlet above what was Derwent village to the Derwent Dam, is not metalled. It provides what is probably the easiest walking amidst lovely surroundings in the entire Peak District. The first stretch, from the viaduct to Derwent, is fairly well-walked—but by no means overcrowded—but north of Derwent the route is invariably peaceful and almost empty. The route runs alongside the water the whole way, with the hills rising steeply to the east and there are few more satisfying views than water glittering and shining when seen through trees. I find this track very useful too in the depth of winter when the road north of Derwent is choked with uncleared snow. From the Derwent Dam to Slippery Stones and back—even with no deviations up Howden Clough or Abbey Brook—is a satisfying walk on a short winter's day.

Having taken care in crossing the busy main road, the track leaves the Ashopton Viaduct very obviously (signed as a bridleway) at the eastern end (no cars are allowed) and runs above the water with delightful woods to the east (watch out for squirrels). I have often seen owls in the vicinity of Grainfoot and a number of duck

have taken up residence (permanently I hope) on the water. Grainfoot Farm is marked on the 2½" O.S. map, but only the ruins remain—if you look carefully. A little further along, where a track goes up to High House—and there is a locked gate—the old Jaggers Route goes up the hillside past Grindle Barn en route for the end of Derwent Edge and Moscar, now a useful route to Derwent Edge. A Jagger was a man who led packhorse ponies laden with salt and other goods across these hills before roads were developed. This is the pack-ponies' route from Cheshire via Edale, Jaggers Clough, Hagg Side, which used to cross the River Derwent at Derwent village over the packhorse bridge. This bridge, as is widely known, was taken down stone by stone, each one numbered, and re-erected at Slippery Stones (note the memorial on it, if you go there). Just below the inlet marked "Derwent" on the O.S. map, lies what was the village. Its houses, Post Office, Hall and church all disappeared when Ladybower was flooded, though the church spire stuck out above the water until 1949, and a strange sight it looked.

The outline of the small village can still be seen in very dry summers, when the reservoir is low, and the sad sight seems to attract hordes of people who wander morbidly among the ruins. The church tower was demolished by explosives in these conditions when it became dangerously unsafe.

From this point to the Derwent Dam, the access-only road is metalled and usually quiet. It runs past the old school, and a farm (Old House) before it dips to curve round under the dam. The track continues more or less level just where the road begins to go down, passing through white painted gates, past a house and on by the water. If the walker leaves his car in the new picnic area at Fairholmes he can by-pass the gate and house by taking the path up through the woods, leaving the road on

# THE VALLEYS
## The main Upper Derwent Valley, Ashopton to the source

the east side of the road's curve under the dam, and continuing past the end of the dam wall and over a stile on to the track.

No route guidance whatsoever is needed from here to Slippery Stones, as the track runs clearly all the way, with only one or two little inclines. I always particularly enjoy the stretch along the upper Derwent Reservoir, and round the bottom of Abbey Brook. There are beautiful views looking back down the reservoir from the track just south of the Howden Dam. Another favourite stretch is from Howden Clough north to Slippery Stones where the water is seen through trees for much of the way. Pause at the bottom of Howden Clough, and look down the rather mysterious inlet. In misty conditions, you could be looking across a Scottish loch or down an arm of the sea in North Devon. I remember walking back down this track after a full day, in darkness with the water shimmering and lapping on the right, and a huge yellow Hunter's moon over the Eastern Edges on the left. Together with the blackness of the silent forest, it was superbly beautiful.

From the lay-by near the Ashopton Viaduct to Slippery Stones via this route is about eight miles and from the Fairholmes car park five and a half, so that somewhere in the vicinity of the Packhorse bridge must be a turning point, except for strong walkers. If you are using the track outwards and return, please remember you have the same number of miles to go back— but there will be no tedium; the views on return are different and just as interesting.

One other point when you do this walk— have a look at the sheer, solid craftsmanship in the construction of the dams and the bridges. Each stone is a minor masterpiece, and the "gateway" at the end of the Howden Dam is magnificent. The bridges over Abbey Brook and Hollin Clough carry water pipes and the rough track, yet they were worth doing and were certainly done well. Think of some of the things built now in steel and concrete, many of them cracked and unsafe in twenty years. These bridges— if left as they are—will still be as good as new in five hundred years—a tribute to the unknown craftsmen who built them.

*Good routes to the tops go off the track; firstly at Abbey (a) up the valley itself and (b) up Abbey Bank for Lost Lad and Back Tor and secondly at Howden Clough for Howden Edge. Please see "Side Cloughs" section for details.*

*Derwent Reservoir in winter*

# THE VALLEYS
## The main Upper Derwent Valley, Ashopton to the source

### NORTH FROM SLIPPERY STONES

Slippery Stones is the point at which the routes up the east and west banks of the reservoirs meet. The walker who has left his car at Fairholmes (Derwent) will probably not have energy for much further exploration northwards, so the obvious point to park for the upper Derwent area is the King's Tree, when traffic restrictions allow (or use the seasonal minibus service). Suggested walks Nos. 12, 13 and 14 start here. The route north has already been described, but is absolutely straightforward over the Linch Clough stepping stones and along the forest track to the Packhorse Bridge.

Slippery Stones is a junction of a number of tracks and paths and a study of the sketch map and O.S. map, is recommended in chosing the route up the valley. Actually it is made quite clear, heading almost due north off the Cut Gate path just past the footbridge over the Cranberry Clough stream. There is a tribute to Fred Heardman in metal set into the woodwork of this footbridge. It was done in 1978 and hasn't been stolen yet, though the signpost Fred erected nearby, towards the end of his life, was stolen within weeks. The track, which is, as always, a shooters' route, runs quietly on to Broadhead Clough (see 'Side Cloughs" for routes to Eastern Edges), where there is a pretty cascade—more impressive after heavy rain.

The section of the river from Broadhead for about one and a half miles to Upper Small Clough is especially beautiful and is highly recommended. It is a true high-moorland stream, twisting in a rocky bed with many pools and waterfalls. Dippers, wagtails and other water-loving birds can be seen in Spring and Summer and—if you are lucky and very quiet—a weasel may peer at you through the heather. Perhaps the best time of the year is autumn, say late October, when the sparse rowan, birches and scrub oak blend with the orange bracken, the bilberry and the heather. (The time for seeing the heather in purple colours is of course earlier, in late August).

The track from Broadhead runs above the river most of the way, affording grandstand views, but it is quite possible to pick a way up the riverside if preferred. It is an excellent area for lounging on hot days. One word of warning; the crossing of Stainery Clough during or just after heavy rain can be impossible. This is not too bad going up the valley, you simply turn back, but, as I know to my cost, coming south it can be disastrous. After a hard, wet day, with thoughts of a dry car less than two easy miles away, to be faced with an uncrossable torrent is very depressing. I have three times had to struggle upstream

# DETAILS OF SLIPPERY STONES JUNCTION
## Map 8

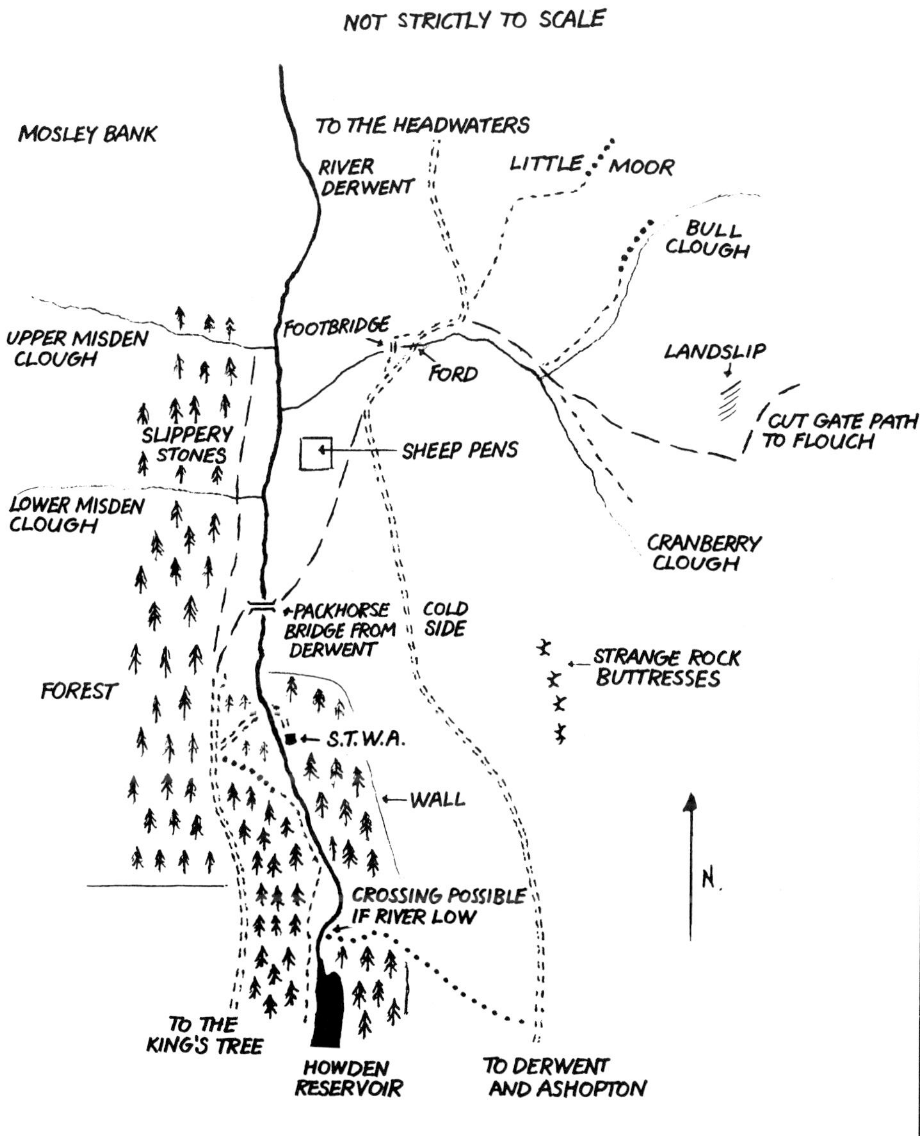

# THE VALLEYS
## The main Upper Derwent Valley, Ashopton to the source

over difficult ground until it could be crossed (on two occasions I had to go right up to the waterfall) and then down the other side again. On no account should any attempt be made to cross until it is safe. Raging water has enormous strength and the attempt is likely to be fatal. If you cross Stainery on a dry summer's day, with the water little more than a trickle, you may think this is exaggerated or fanciful, but I assure you it isn't. (See Stainery Clough for route to Eastern Edges in pleasanter circumstances).

Almost opposite Upper Small Clough, by the tiny Lands Clough, the track ends, though the 2½ inch O.S. map inaccurately shows it ending at Stainery Clough. A vague path continues going rather precariously down to the river's edge west of Humber Knoll. It follows the stream to Coldwell Clough—note the fine pool just south of the side clough. From Coldwell to Hoar, the path by the river side is wet and marshy except in very dry weather, and it is usually better to use the erratic path a little way up the hillside. From Hoar Clough northwards to the point where the valley narrows and turns westward, the path is reasonably clear, twisting about a bit and wet in only one or two places. This is a splendid lonely stretch, savour it as you go, with high hills all around, and no sign that man has ever existed (not quite true). Note the amazing meanderings of the river and the several examples of where it has changed course through the centuries.

If you are going to Fiddler's Green, or returning south via Outer Edge, turn north up Hoar Clough. (See Side Cloughs and chapter on the Tops). If you are bound for Barrow Stones, and do not wish to go as far as the headwaters, turn up Barrow Clough or up the hillside as indicated on the map.

At the point where the river turns in a westerly direction, the valley changes in character, and becomes Narrow and V-shaped for about 300 yards. It is quite practicable to walk, or at least scramble, up the river bed except in times of high water, but the better route is on the path up the hillside to the north. The connection between the waterside path, and this one higher up has never been really established, and it is necessary to scramble up the steep hillside for about 100 feet to join it, just before the river turns.

The valley soon widens again into the huge amphitheatre which is really the Derwent's source. This is a wild, and many people would say—with some justification especially on a grey November day—a melancholy place. But it has its own strange attraction for some as an area of sheer, brooding desolation—and it can be attractive in another mood in Spring sunshine, with curlew and golden plover calling.

The best ways out are as follows:

(a) For the Etherow Valley in the Salter's Brook area, head north over the heather for Swains Head. From there, the course is due north down Far Small Clough to the valley.

(b) For Black Clough, or Bleaklow Stones or perhaps Grinah Stones, but see (c) below, head westerly as soon as the valley ceases to be V-shaped and after the first real stream is crossed. There is no continuous path but make your way across to the rather more pronounced gully which heads south-west. Climb steeply alongside this on the western side—and subsequently in the gully itself. The gully shortly turns south and at this point if you are making for Black Clough, turn due west over rough ground. Otherwise continue due south up the gully until the summit peat groughs are reached. If Bleaklow Stones are the objective, turn south-west when you reach the line of stakes, and follow them over abominable peat groughs with the Stones clearly visible ahead. This route is not recommended in mist and an error in navigation could be awkward—use your compass. For Grinah Stones continue due

# THE VALLEYS
## The main Upper Derwent Valley, Ashopton to the source

south, and if you are on course, you will over-run the northerly head-waters of Deep Grain (over the watershed). There is one clear and deep gully which permits of easy walking until the Bleaklow Stones to Grinah path is reached—then turn east—or west.

(c) For Grinah Stones direct, use Swain's Greave which is usually accepted as the ultimate source of the Derwent. Begin by following the main stream, across jumbled ground, but due south to the rocky gully itself. The best route is up the gully—a bit of a scramble until the peat stage is reached. The great thing to remember here, especially in mist, is that Grinah is due south. Trust the compass and proceed.

(d) For Barrow Stones, choose the first main gully on the left, i.e. east, before you get to the main confluence. This is a very useful route, and quite safe in thick mist, since it is straight and leads unerringly to Barrow Stones.

### FRED HEARDMAN

I have mentioned the name of Fred Heardman and would like to add a little here about that wonderful man. When I first got to know him in the early 50's he was landlord of "The Nag's Head" in Edale and I suppose middle-aged. He had been, and indeed still was a great walker (and a great "trespasser" in the pre-access days). Even more, perhaps, he was a great observer and a lover of the solitude. He would take considerable pains to help young people on the hills, and indeed was the founder of the Peak Park's Information Service. I remember one early evening in "The Nag's Head", when two young lads timidly came in (they did in those days) and enquired about camping (this was long before Field Head and the other camping fields). Fred had no hesitation in leaving his busy bar and spending 10 minutes describing the area and where they could best camp. I used to meet him occasionally at Peak Park meetings, and more frequently on Kinder and Bleaklow—almost always alone—like me—and it was always a great pleasure and privilege to talk to him. Someone once said to me that when you had gained the friendship of Fred, you had done something worthwhile and that was true.

There are two "memorials" to him—one a rather strange plantation on the path to the Nab in Edale, and the other a little plaque on the wooden footbridge crossing Cranberry Clough at Slippery Stones. Most of those who knew him prefer perhaps to remember that kind, courteous gentleman wandering quietly over the lonely hills.

# THE VALLEYS
## The main Upper Derwent Valley, Ashopton to the source

*Derwent in winter*

## THE SIDE CLOUGHS

Both the Derwent and Westend valleys have a number of side cloughs which vary greatly in character, and are well worthy of exploration, either as a route to the ridges or for an hour's pleasant walking. The Alport, being a deep incised valley, cut into the gritstone layers, has few side cloughs and none of these few, except perhaps Nether Reddale, provides any exciting exploration.

As I have said, the cloughs vary considerably in character, but they have one thing in common: their interest lies in the section from the main valley to the point where they cease to be a real valley in their own right and debouch onto the moors into a series of peaty groughs, which are their water-gathering grounds.

One interesting difference, not easy to explain, is that whereas some are almost straight—for example Linch Clough—others exhibit a perfect example of what geographers call interlocking spurs. Look down Cranberry Clough from Howden Edge and you will see exactly what I mean. Some additionally are lightly wooded with birch, scrub oak and rowan in the lower regions. On a sunny day in May, Bull Clough or Stainery Clough are intimate fairy glens, utterly different from the stern moors above. In some cases the stream has scarcely cut through the first eastern escarpment (like Hoar Clough) so that the valley is short and the walker soon reaches the peat grough stage. One—Abbey Brook—has penetrated a long way, forming a deep gorge through the main escarpment with extensive headwaters (I have included this as a side clough, though it could almost be thought of as a valley in its own right).

40

# CHAPTER 2

# THE UPPER DERWENT VALLEY

# SIDE CLOUGHS EAST OF THE RIVER

## ABBEY BROOK

This is by far the longest and largest of the side valleys on the eastern side and can be highly recommended. I have walked up and down it hundreds of times in sun, mist, snow and all the variations, but always with intense enjoyment. It is a valley to calm the soul and lighten the heart.

The actual course of the river is interesting. The headwaters start within yards of Howden Edge to the north, converging and flowing east then south-east for all the world as though they were to join Hobson Moss Dike and the River Loxley. But the stream is turned south by the high ground extending from Back Tor. It then breaks through the Edge in what is, I think, the most dramatic gorge in the High Peak. It is very steep-sided, sheer in many places, with a lot of crag, and impressive waterfalls in the stream. After a fairly short distance, the water is turned to the west by a gritstone spur, in which general direction it runs for the rest of its course. Just west of this final turn, the stream is joined by the waters of Sheepfold Clough and the area of the confluence is interesting. There are several humps which at first sight seem to be difficult to account for. There is no doubt, I think, that they are caused by changes in the courses of the streams. Thousands of years ago, the main stream must have swung somewhat further south, joining the Sheepfold Clough stream, approximately where the old cabins stood. At some stage, in great flood, it must have switched to its present course, cutting

# THE VALLEYS
## The Upper Derwent Valley, the side cloughs east of the river

down greatly to form the present deeply incised gorge. It will be noted that Sheepfold Clough runs at an appreciably higher level than that of the main stream.

Until about 20 years ago, two shooting cabins stood at the bottom of Sheepfold Clough, one on either side of the stream. (The presence of the cabins was the reason for the track to that point up from the Derwent Valley). The one to the east of the stream disintegrated, helped considerably by the vandals, and it is quite difficult now to see even the foundations on which it stood. The second cabin lasted longer, and its death was prolonged. It was repaired in the 1960's but the weather and vandalism combined to bring about its destruction. Even in 1975 it provided some shelter, but now it is no more, just a few stones and some unsightly rusty corrugated iron. A great pity—it provided me, and no doubt many other walkers, with welcome shelter on many a bitter day.

## ROUTES

As always, any route is possible once open country is reached, and those given here are what the writer thinks the best for interest, views and reasonable going. Do keep to paths until access land is reached.

Actually, it is more rewarding scenically to walk down Abbey Brook rather than up, but since most walkers will approach from Derwent and the reservoir track, the route is given in that direction. The way starts just after the reservoir track begins to dip to cross Abbey Brook itself, and goes at 45 degrees for a short way, almost over the remains of a farm, indeed the floor tiles of a room are still visible. This is a lovely spot at any time, but especially in Spring, when there is a host of daffodils, and snowdrops—please do not pick them.

The track quickly turns uphill through the forest gate and then turns again left at 90 degrees for the valley. (The track going uphill should be ignored). It runs alongside the forest for a time, through a gate—with a stile—and on quite clearly, before dipping to an unnamed side clough. There is another—and older—route up to this point, which starts obscurely in the trees to the south of the stream, and runs gloomily up to emerge near the gate and stile mentioned above. It then goes parallel to the main track on the other side of the wall, dipping to the unnamed clough. There is not a lot to be said for this alternative except that it is more mysterious and provides a measure of stillness on days of gale or high wind.

After crossing the side clough, the track is very plain, climbing across the hillside. The views into the valley, with scattered trees on the far hillside are very attractive, especially in spring, and the line of high edges ahead either spurs the feet, or depresses the heart—it depends on how you look at it. The track throws height away to cross Cogman Clough (annoying coming the other way at the end of a tiring day) and climbs round the spur before levelling. Take this section gently, with many backward glances at the beautiful view down the valley to the reservoir and beyond to Birchinlee. The track is now nearer the stream and high above it in a perfect V-shaped—i.e. water cut—valley. It is a very attractive section: pause frequently to admire the waterfalls in Gravy Clough (strange name) and the grey crag of Berristers Tor. The track, climbing gently, swings somewhat away from the main stream to "the cabins", which is a sort of Abbey Clapham Junction of routes, as follows:

(a) For Lost Lad and a return to the reservoir via Abbey Bank, the route turns south for a time and is much less clear. If in difficulty, or the track is lost, make for Lost Lad Hillend, which (unless in cloud) is clearly visible ahead. Under Lost Lad Hillend the track (more a path really) turns west and becomes more plain. A diversion can be made involving more climbing, to the top of Lost Lad, a really excellent viewpoint. If views are the object of the

# THE VALLEY OF ABBEY BROOK
## Map 9

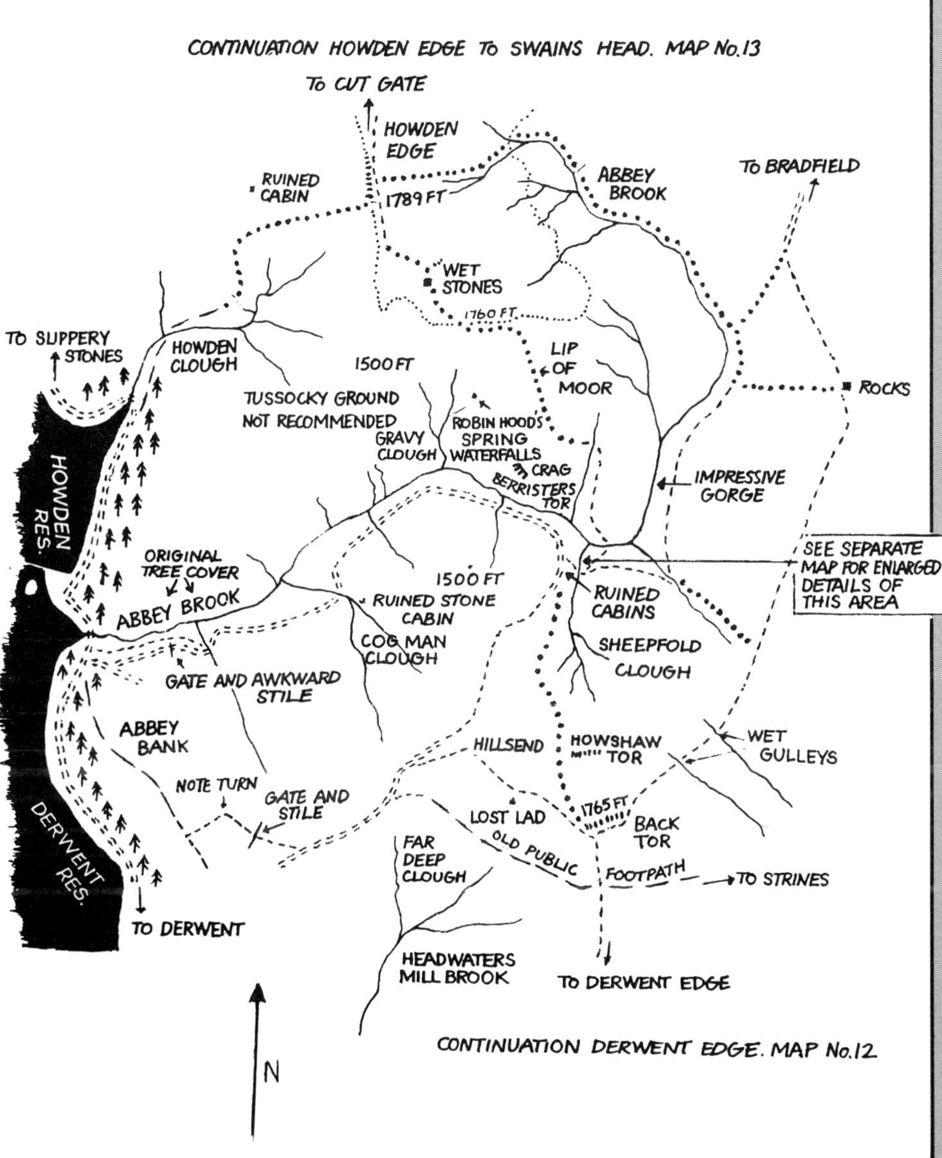

exercise, this point is highly recommended — a much better spot than the somewhat higher, and better known Back Tor half a mile away. A small monument has recently been erected alongside the cairn to a walker who loved the area, and although memorials on high ground are generally to be discouraged, this usefully indicates the directions of the various hills to be seen.

Back to Lost Lad Hillend. From here, the track, little more than two wheel ruts, is soon joined by the path from Strines. It runs south-west for a short way, before turning north-west. A track continues south-west so make sure you turn — a good guide is the fence, with a gate on the right and a cumbersome up and over stile to the left of it. The path runs almost due north-west now, with an awkward little turn left (west) down the hillside after a short distance, before resuming its north westerly direction. A stone marked "Path" indicates the left turn. In mist, don't worry if you over-run the turn — continue north-west and you will reach the same spot, on reasonably good ground. This is one of the "best descents" (see page 53) and the views are beautiful, down to the Derwent reservoir, and ahead to the Howden and the continuing Derwent Valley. Highly recommended.

(b) For Back Tor direct. This is quite a difficult mile, with no path — a question of picking your way, almost due south. The "best" route perhaps is to the west of Sheepfold Clough, and across the splayed water courses to Howshaw Tor, where, if you are lucky, you will pick up a vague and peaty path to Back Tor looming obviously ahead.

(c) For the Abbey Brook headquarters (and Howden Edge) or Duke's Road to Bradfield, or the circle round to Back Tor. Cross Sheepfold Clough by the ruined cabin, pick up the path going round the hump, and proceed upwards due east on a narrow path running across and up the steep hillside. There is a change of direction to slightly east of north at the small side clough (where you may continue east across the open moor to pick up the path to be mentioned shortly) and the route continues on the very lip of the hill, above the river, until the gorge ends and becomes a normal high-ground stream. The whole of this stretch is impressive, with superb views into the canyon and rock scenery almost the equal of the Lake District. The stream too is attractive, with many waterfalls. Unless the water is high, it is possible to pick a way up or alongside the stream bed, but the route on the hillside is superior. A word of warning; although the path is clear, make sure you put your feet down firmly. A slip and fall almost anywhere on it could be disastrous, with you ending up dead or badly injured in the river. Just before the gorge ends, for example, the side is sheer, although this cannot be seen from the path. The path is more difficult to follow after the gorge. If you are making a circle round to Back Tor, it is best to pick a way across to the obvious rocks where a reasonably good path is joined. If you want the Duke's Road, go straight ahead following the east bank and as the stream turns westwards, walk across to pick up the track. Neither is particularly recommended in mist as it is easier to over-run the paths. Even in mist, the route back to Howden Edge is easy to follow. Stay with the stream like a leech. There is a sketchy path on the north side of it — off and on. As the definite stream bed deteriorates into peat groughs, walk due west to reach Howden Edge. This section is over rough ground, (unless you are lucky enough to find a faint path). If the cloud is down, don't panic if it seems to take a long time to reach the edge. On the map it looks a very short section, but on the desolation of the dip slope it seems a long way. Be sure of one thing, due west will bring you to your destination.

(d) For Howden Edge direct. Begin for the first few yards as though on route (c), but

# DETAILS OF RUINED CABINS AREA ABBEY BROOK
## Map 10

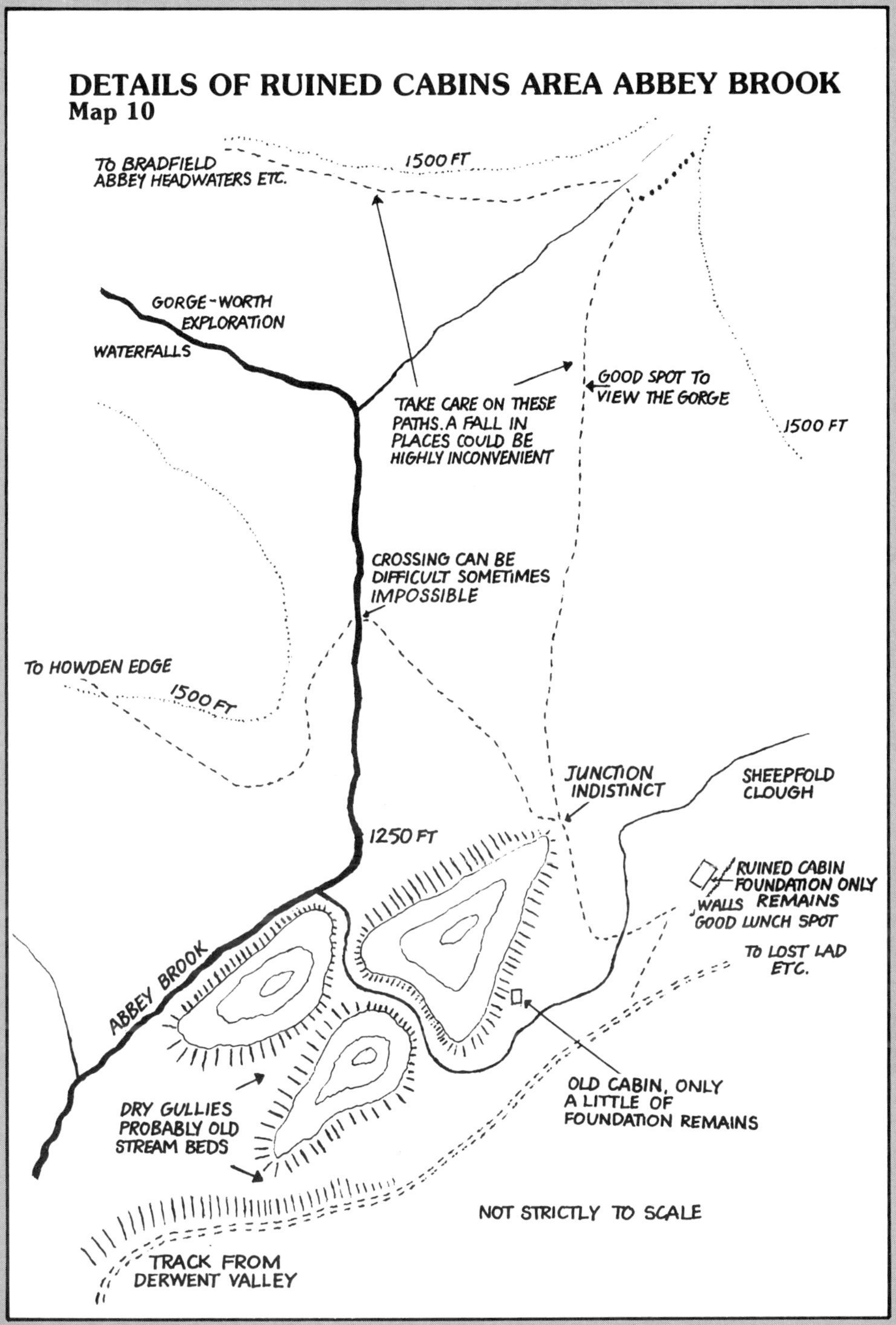

# THE VALLEYS
## The Upper Derwent Valley, the side cloughs east of the river

in the first gap, instead of going up, go down across the hillside to the stream, which must be crossed. Note: during or after heavy rain, melting snow etc., the stream may be uncrossable. Check lower down before starting this route. A faint path goes up and across the hillside above Foul Clough. Pause on this, firstly perhaps to rest and secondly to absorb the glorious views westward down the valley. The faint path crosses Foul Clough, high up, and then disappears. It is possible to strike directly for Wet Stones from here, but the best route is to follow the edge in two bulges. The going is better and the views far superior. Below is the romantically named Robin Hood's Spring. Wet Stones are a sound navigational guide in mist on a featureless hillside. At least you know where you are! A tricky bit comes after Wet Stones too. Although the route is generally northerly, it is necessary to walk north-west for 200 yards in order to pick up a reasonable path up a rough shallow channel, leading to the little cairn at the highest point of the Edge called High Stones. From then on the route is easy (see Eastern Edges).

## HOWDEN CLOUGH

This walk can be a pleasant hour's diversion from the reservoir track, or can be used en route for Howden Edge. A clear firm path is shown on the Dark Peak 2½ inch map, running across to Cut Gate, but do not be misled. Beyond the head of the clough no such path exists and the going, via Penistone Stile, is rough. The path veers off the reservoir track just short of the bridge and goes for some way through the forest, climbing gently. Where it emerges is a delightful spot—have a rest there—spend three hours there if it is a hot summer's day. There will probably be no sound except for the streams. The path crosses the brook and climbs across the hillside. A short way up is a small dam and reservoir. I have not been able to discover why it was built, but have a theory that it originally provided water storage for Howden House and the old farm in the valley before flooding.

As the path turns north round the spur, it becomes obscure. If bound for Howden Edge, it is best to follow the north-pointing arm of the stream, but keeping well clear of it to avoid the very wet ground, reeds, tussocks etc. Turn east on the drier

UPPER DERWENT VALLEY

# THE VALLEYS
## The Upper Derwent Valley, the side cloughs east of the river

*Upper Derwent*

ground, round the headwaters, and tackle the very steep slope to Howden Edge, choosing a route keeping mainly to grass. Stops for a rest will not be wearisome as the views westwards and southwards are superb. If it is a warm spring day, you may see little lizards darting in the heather.

An alternative and easier route up to the Edge, is to take the path just past the dam and an area of very wet ground, climbing less steeply on the north side of the stream, east south-east, and up to Row Top, finishing beside a ruined wall. This route is drier and less arduous.

The area of Long Edge is not recommended. It is tussocky and the going is awful. The shooting cabin marked on the O.S. map is quite difficult to find and in any case is little more than a heap of stones affording no shelter.

## CRANBERRY CLOUGH

This attractive little valley will probably be explored for its own sake, since the Cut Gate path is an easier route to the tops. However, I often use it as a much quieter alternative. The normal path for Gate Cut is used from the packhorse bridge, but after crossing the water of Bull Clough, while

the Cut Gate path ascends steeply up the spur, take what was once merely a sheep path up the side of the stream. It is quite easy going, with pretty waterfalls and scattered trees of birch and scrub oak. Almost every yard invites a rest on the soft grass to absorb the silence and peace of the scene. Just past the first small side stream from the left, whilst a path of sorts continues lower down, it is best to climb up the hillside to join another clearer path, still going upstream, but higher. Turn left at the main junction up Little Cranberry Clough; (other routes east and south are possible, but are not really recommended as the going is rough and can be tiresome). A little further on, the clough loses its character and, if the walker is bound for Cut Gate, there is a rough and wet 300 yards, heading due north. No definite route can be advised—pick your way and avoid the marsh by going round it unless the weather has been dry. After this poor stretch, the rest is a pleasant walk up the dry and mainly grassy hillside. Try to visit this area in May or June. There are nearly always one or two pairs of curlew which nest in the vast amphitheatre under Margery Hill and Howden Edge and their wild, sad call is music to any hill walker.

*Cold Side Oaks to King's Tree*

# THE VALLEYS
## The Upper Derwent Valley, the side cloughs east of the river

### STAINERY CLOUGH

This is quite a long clough, with headwaters extending beyond the first escarpment (Crow Stones Edge) to the higher Outer Edge. The lower reaches are pretty, with quite a lot of trees, mainly scrub oak, birches and rowan. The central section still provides interesting exploration with the stream in a rocky bed and loneliness all round. The area above the waterfall is best left alone—a region of peat groughs, deep heather and difficult going.

Until the last ten years or so, there was no path up the clough. More recently a rough and rather intermittent path—although not a legal right of way—has developed on the east side of the stream. (A strange bit of orientation here. Walking up and down the Derwent Valley, I had the feeling for years that, since Stainery Cross goes off to the right going upstream, it must run east. But the Derwent has turned west here, so that the start of Stainery runs almost due north). To return; the path has developed, but is still pretty rough, crossing boulders in places, and higher up plunging about in the heather above the water. It eventually disappears and the more persevering walker is left to forge a rather difficult course up the stream bed or through the rough vegetation alongside. The going becomes more rocky—and steeper—so that only the more hardy will reach the waterfall. A better route really is to abandon the valley bottom somewhere near Horse Stone Spring, and pick a way up through the somewhat easier and drier ground on the north-west side.

*Generally speaking the clough can best be recommended for its attractive lower reaches.*

### COLDWELL CLOUGH

This is a short V-shaped cleft running north-east from the Derwent towards Hoar Stones. It is not really a good route to anywhere, and there is no reasonable path.

The best route is up on the northern bank, but it involves pushing through bracken (in summer) and heather, without a great deal of reward, though the watercourse is quite attractive.

### HOAR CLOUGH

Useful as a route from the Derwent Valley to Langsett, and perhaps Fiddlers Green—navigation is reasonably easy, but it is scarcely a clough at all, though very quiet. Its chief attraction is the tumble of rocks down the stream from the little waterfall. Access is quite easy as, although there is no continuous path, the ground on both sides is fairly dry and not too tangled.

### BULL CLOUGH

Walkers not given to more detailed exploration, will be acquainted with Bull Clough (though they may not know its name) through looking down on to the attractive stream from the well-trodden Cut Gate path. It is a short but pleasant little valley, with a pretty section in the area of the stream junction and it provides a quiet climb up to Bull Stones, joining the Eastern Edges route.

A faint path leads left at 45 degrees off the Cut Gate path from Slippery Stones, just short of the stream crossing. It continues vaguely on the north side, above the stream to begin with, and later descending into it. There is no clear route, and you will have to pick your way through some wet and rough patches, though there are no real difficulties. Where the clough turns somewhat easterly, there is an attractive area with trees and sparkling water—a pleasant spot for a ten minute rest. Take your choice of either bank from here, but if you are heading for Bull Stones, the northern side is best, and higher up it becomes reasonably dry walking.

# THE VALLEYS
## The Upper Derwent Valley, the side cloughs east of the river

*Abbey Clough*

## BROADHEAD CLOUGH

As the name suggests, and in complete contrast with, say, Cranberry Clough, after the first 200 yards of steep sides, the clough opens out to a curved hillside, like half a basin, rising to the edge. I find it a hillside of great beauty, perhaps because of the varied vegetation—bracken, bilberry, heather, grasses, mosses etc. It is at its best on a late summer evening of mellow sunshine, when the colours blend to provide a glorious mosaic, and the peace of the scene makes you hold your breath. I remember so many descents from Crow Stones at the end of a perfect day on the hills, when I felt it a great privilege to have been allowed that moment of perfection.

This clough was used greatly in the past for shooting, as witness the two cabins which used to stand on the north side, and the number of clear paths leading up from the valley. One of the long dead shooters was presumably Lord Edward Howard, since a nearby spring is so named after him. It is still used for shooting but the cabins are no more. However, one of the paths provides an excellent way up to the Edge. The clear path going across the hillside leaves the track up the Derwent Valley 200 yards before it crosses the stream. It runs above the water for a short way, with lovely views up the Derwent, and then crosses a side stream. From then on, the ascent is fairly steep and the path not too clear, but it runs roughly up the line of shooting butts, to the edge of the peat cover. It doesn't matter a great deal, as there is no difficulty in picking a route almost anywhere on the hillside. The views west, north and south, from the top are superb, and you might see a mountain hare wandering amongst the rocks. In a grough just over the top, are the remains of the light aircraft mentioned in the chapter on the Eastern Edges.

# CHAPTER 3

# THE UPPER DERWENT VALLEY

# SIDE CLOUGHS

# WEST OF THE RIVER

*Hagg Farm*

◄ *Ashop Valley*

## OUZELDEN CLOUGH

An interesting name. Presumably the dean or dene (a narrow valley) was a noted haunt of the ring ouzel, which can still be seen in the area.

The clough runs west off the reservoir road starting from the inlet in the Derwent Reservoir, a mile north from the dam. After half a mile the valley divides, Ouzelden Clough continuing westward and Alport Grain running south and west. There is no access into Ouzelden Clough.

## LINCH CLOUGH

Since Linch Clough starts at the stepping stones, only yards from the King's Tree roundabout, one would think that the first section at least, where there is a very good path, would be widely visited; but not so. Even on glorious hot early evenings in summer, as I have come off the ridge expecting strollers or picnic parties, the valley has invariably been empty.

The easy path leads off to the left just past the crossing of the stream and goes through the trees for a short way before passing through the wall. I have seen red squirrels here—not for some time I'm afraid. After a few more yards uphill, the path (an old shooters' path) levels for three hundred yards. Pause here for a moment and look ahead at the V of the clough against the sky. It seems to invite the question "What is beyond?" I was once standing so, many years ago, when I was joined by a charming man in a black city suit and thin highly-polished shoes. He told me he was on his way to Manchester for a conference, but having three hours to spare, he had turned off the Snake Road and driven as far as the King's Tree. He was a city man through and through and the hills of Britain were an alien world, as unknown as the Andes are to me. Yet he was fascinated. What, he asked me, was beyond that V? What was ahead where the water lead? I tried to give him some idea of the splendours of the view from Grinah; the roof of the world feeling of the ridges. He sighed—it was a different world from the one he inhabited, and he returned sadly, perhaps, to his car and I think he envied me my day up there in the solitude—instead of sitting round a table in a stuffy office in Manchester. I certainly didn't envy him, though he was no doubt far, far richer.

Most walkers using Linch Clough will be heading for Ronksley and Barrow or Grinah Stones. The Clough itself is

# THE VALLEYS
## The Upper Derwent Valley, the side cloughs west of the river

extremely steep-sided all the way, which precludes walking up the sides (except with great difficulty, or for people with one leg shorter than the other). Thus, the only pleasant routes are those climbing out of or the one going up the stream.

What appears to be the easiest route out of the valley is the old shooters' path (not marked on the 2½ inch map) climbing across the north side and starting only a few yards from the emergence from the forest. It goes half-right and proceeds pleasantly up the main climb but then—here's the rub—it fades, and leaves the walker with some rough heathery miles to the top of Ronksley. Not really to be recommended.

All in all, a better route out is to follow the shooters' path along the level, across the stream, from which point the path—still clear but not shown on the map—doubles back south-east, climbing across the hillside. After some wet patches higher up, it turns south but in this area unfortunately fades away. The walker is left with a tussocky half mile, moving north-west to the good going at the "end" of Ronksley. An alternative is to leave this path part way up the southern hillside, and climb **very** steeply, when he will eventually reach much better going and not so much incline, at the end of an old wall. On a bright sunny morning, when you are impatient to be on the airy ridge, this is the route to choose.

The route up the stream is much easier in gradient and is a delightful stretch with the gurgling water playing games all the way. As I frequently have to say, until recently there was no sign of a path, but over the last few years a sketchy, intermittent one has developed. In parts the best route is immediately alongside the water; sometimes it is better to use old sheep tracks a short way up the hillside. It is impossible to give a step by step guide, but the hill walker will, I'm quite sure, pick his way happily. One word of warning—there

are one or two sections where a fall or stumble could result in a nasty accident so watch what you're doing. As the stream gets to the peat grough stage, take an obvious left forking gully, and you should pick up a faint path heading due west, taking you to the large shooting butt on the Ronksley route.

## LOWER SMALL CLOUGH

This clough provides a useful route on to Ronksley from the Derwent Valley. It leaves the valley, running south-west, just north of Deer Holes at a delightful watersmeet. I have spent hours sitting there, drinking in the serenity. I remember once, on a sunny morning in May, watching a pair of wrens darting about in their strange, quick fashion. It seemed an alien habitat for them so far up the valley, though I have seen wrens even higher, but they seemed entirely happy.

There is only one good route. It starts steeply up the little spur on the north-west side, and a faint path continued climbing gently on that side, meandering pleasantly through the bracken above the stream. There are no difficulties, except that the path later becomes rather peaty. There is a line of shooting butts on each side and eventually the beautifully hidden cabin is reached. The going from there is more peaty; either up the deep, and often wet, peat channel, or through the heather on the top sides until the Ronksley route is reached.

I'm not proposing to tell many hill-navigation stories in this book, as they tend to be boring to others, but I shall allow myself one here. I was once walking—strolling would be a better word—up Lower Small Clough fairly late in the afternoon, when I met a party of four soldiers. They were all dressed in camouflage uniforms, the leader being about 35 years of age and the others young, perhaps nineteen or twenty. The

# THE VALLEYS
## The Upper Derwent Valley, the side cloughs west of the river

older man was laden with all the right equipment, maps etc., and asked in a very self-assured voice if I had seen any of "his lads" at Grinah Stones—pointing ahead as he came down the clough, to Horse Stone. I said I hadn't seen any soldiers at all, but pointed out that the rock across the valley wasn't Grinah. This he wouldn't have at any price, and flatly contradicted me. After some discussion when I pointed out other rocky landmarks, and finally convinced him I did know these hills, he more meekly asked where Grinah Stones were. I pointed in that direction, indicating that he was more than 90 degrees off-course. I have rarely seen a man so deflated. He faced near rebellion from the three young soldiers (who were tired and had slumped in the heather) when he shamefacedly indicated they had to retrace their steps. I sat down for five minutes to allow him to withdraw with some sort of dignity, and the last I saw was of the small group wearily climbing the hillside in their own footmarks.

## UPPER SMALL CLOUGH

This little valley leaves the Derwent a quarter of a mile north-west from Lower Small Clough and like the latter goes south-west. Its use is as a route to Round Hill, when the northern bank should be followed, but this cannot really be recommended as the going is rough, and Lower Small Clough is much superior.

## BARROW CLOUGH

A quiet clough, high in the hills, where the presence of any other human being is most unlikely. It can be used as a route to Round Hill or Barrow Stones, though many walkers will prefer the open hillside to the north for the climb.

The clough leaves the Derwent Valley, a little west of Hoar Clough, and runs slightly west of south—though I always have the feeling, when walking up, that I am going west. There is a faint path, which becomes even fainter, on the west side, until the steep peat gullies are reached. From that point, Round Hill is due south over the heather and Barrow Stones are due west. In clear conditions, there is no mistaking the latter as the Crown Stone is prominent—but the heather is rather thick in places.

# THE WESTEND VALLEY
## Map 11

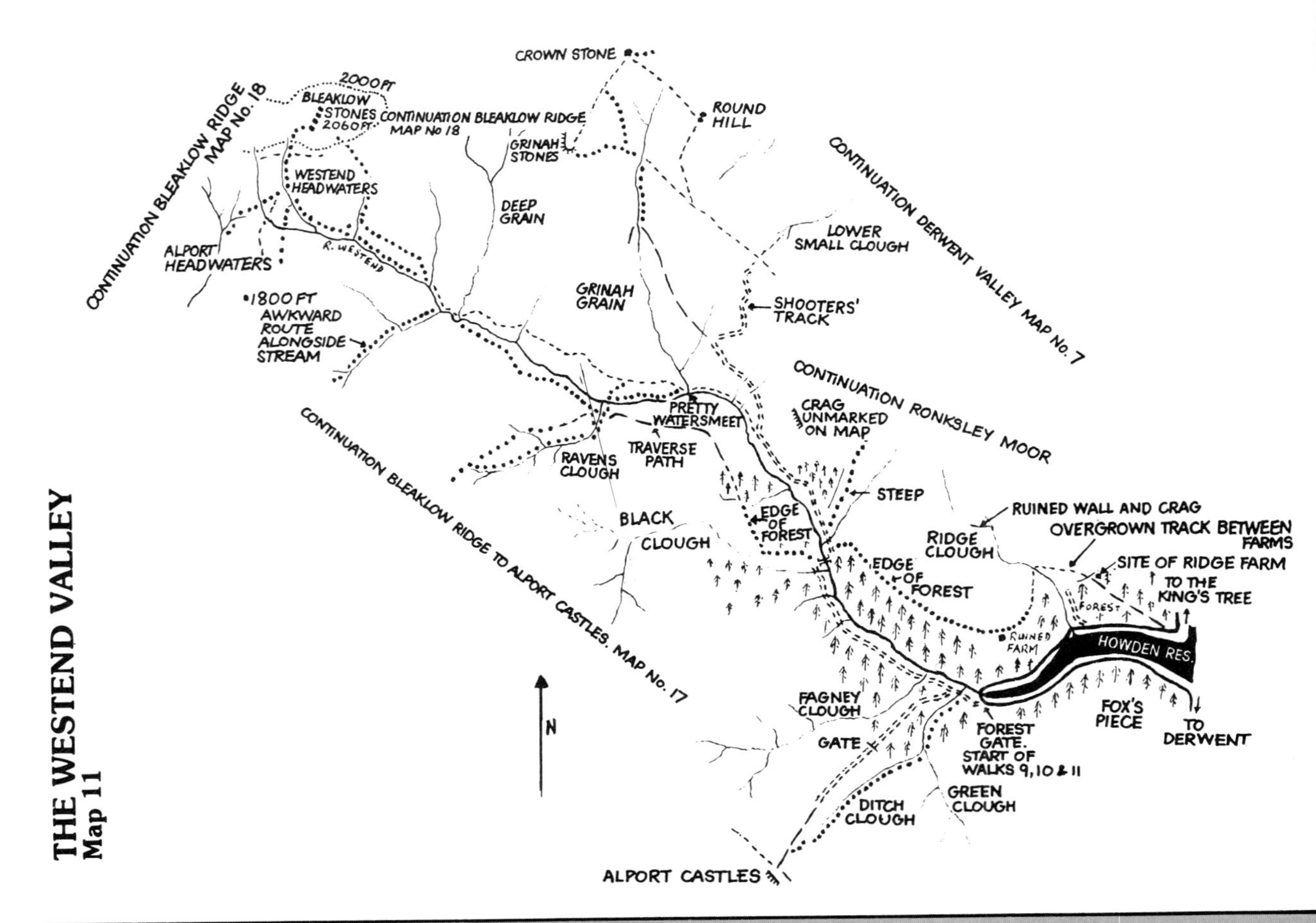

# CHAPTER 4

# THE WESTEND VALLEY

# INCLUDING SIDE CLOUGHS

## THE MAIN VALLEY

The River Westend is the main tributary of the Derwent in the northern sector. It rises at Westend Head, just west of Bleaklow Stones and originally joined the Derwent about 5 miles away near Howden House. The last mile of the valley was flooded in 1912 and is now the long westward pointing arm of the Howden Reservoir.

For the walker seeking quietness and serenity the valley is a delight, and the going easy. However, although the valley is quite well-used by the public, there is no public footpath into it nor any access agreement. The river falls 1,100 feet in its 4 mile journey—from about 2,000 feet in the high peat gullies to 900 feet where it joins the reservoir—so that the water is fast and free, with plenty of waterfalls and water slides. There is also great contrast in scenery. From the quiet forest at the start, to the open curving valley near Grinah Grain, on to the final delightful mile where the stream comes down from the high moors. Until the junction with Deep Grain, the valley is surprisingly wide, with none of the gorge-like qualities of the Alport.

A shooters' track runs up the first section, climbing eventually on to Ronksley, with some hair-raising gradients (this track is erroneously shown on the 2½ inch O.S. map as ending in Grinah Grain) and provides very easy access. For the not-too serious walker, who wants a couple of hours of pleasant strolling in quiet semi-wild conditions, this track is the ideal answer.

Normally, all walks will start through the forest gate at the very end of the reservoir arm, just before the bridge and suggested walks Nos. 9, 10 and 11 start here. Limited parking for a few cars is available close in to the steep grassy bank on the left (but not on Bank Holidays or summer Sundays when the traffic scheme is in operation). For nearly a mile, the track closely follows the river through the forest.

# THE VALLEYS
## The Westend Valley, including side cloughs

It is a beautiful stretch. Many times on Saturday mornings, after a hectic week's work with its attendant noise and fret, I have stood near the water—just absorbing the silence. It is a favourite area for squirrels too. Years ago I have seen red ones, but for some years now only grey. I know they are supposed to be pests, but they are very attractive to watch. A year or so ago, one showed surprising aggression, when I walked towards the tree it had just raced up. It turned round on a branch, not really far away, and defied me to approach with a series of harsh barking noises, and no fear. Presumably it was defending its nearby drey (winter 'nest').

A couple of hundred yards along from the gate, and just over the water of Ditch Clough, the clear and sign-posted route (the only legal right of way crossing the valley), to Alport Castles (a natural rock formation) climbs straight up the hillside. It is a quick and easy route to the tops, the first part through the trees (with tantalising glimpses of Grinah Stones to the north) then up open moorland on a spur between Ditch and Fagney Cloughs, to the top. For anyone with only about two hours to spare, who wants to have a taste of the moors—with spectacular views—this path to Alport Castles and back is highly recommended. It is steep but easy, and the fact that you will return the same way is no disadvantage as the views are different and the descent is one of the best in the area. From the top (don't go straight ahead and fall over the edge—its a long way down) the view north to Bleaklow, west to Kinder, east to the Edges and south to a variety of hills, is superb. There's a nice wall to shelter under too, if the wind is blowing strong and cold.

*(Please see appropriate chapter of "The Tops" for ridge walks).*

Back to the valley! At the bottom of Fagney Clough is the site of Westend Farm—long since vanished; vanished indeed so completely that it is very difficult even to guess as to where the buildings actually stood. They must have been near the stream—for drinking water—and there is only one flattish area, but no stones remaining; perhaps they were carted away and used elsewhere. The track from here to the bridge is lovely. Pause frequently to look at the views upstream, which are far more reminiscent of the Highlands of

# THE VALLEYS
## The Westend Valley, including side cloughs

Scotland than of Derbyshire. The water is a typical mountain or high moorland stream with lots of rock and plenty of noise and movement. The mysterious trees come right down to the water's edge—many pleasant picnic spots, but great care needed with smoking, and no fires please.

Just beyond the foot of Black Clough, the track crosses the river to the east bank, on a wooden bridge lately reinforced by steel girders—take care when using this bridge. On the left, just before the crossing is a clearing where the shooters gather after the day and sort out the spoils. This was presumably the site of Blacklow Court marked on the maps. The forest, more recently planted, continues for a time, but the track is more open and it can be followed without the slightest difficulty. After just over half a mile the track begins to climb across the eastern hillside (the 2½ inch O.S. map is not entirely accurate) and here two possible routes are available:

1. **To follow the track up on to Ronksley, with an alternative path up Grinah Grain; or**
2. **To continue on a faint path by the side of the Westend.**

Let's take 1. first. The track climbs, fairly gently at first, then more steeply across Dry Clough to a point above Grinah Grain. From there it turns abruptly and steeply up the hillside in a general zig-zag to reach the top of the ridge (where the track ends) opposite the head of Lower Small Clough. There is no difficulty whatever to that point, but please see "Ronksley" for ridge routes.

From the point where the track turns steeply east, a fairly faint path continues for a time up the east side of Grinah Grain. The junction is not all that clear, but if necessary a little casting about will find it. It might be more difficult in mist. This path runs due north, with the water below gradually getting closer as the valley rises, until eventually the path descends and crosses the stream and turns back on itself before becoming lost in the vegetation of Ridgewalk Moor. Most walkers will be heading for Grinah or Barrow Stones, and no route from here on is really easy. The best way, I think, is to continue, picking your way, on the east side, until you are high enough to see Grinah to the west—a small depression also comes in from the east at this point. From there onwards, it is a matter of choosing the driest route

# THE VALLEYS
## The Westend Valley, including side cloughs

possible upwards. There are some wet bits, but keep to the grass as far as possible, and take advantage of the faint paths (some of them sheep paths) which are available. It is best to move somewhat to the left across the hillside towards the rocks, where the grass runs in corridors. In mist it's much more difficult!

*Please see section on "The Tops" for routes from Grinah.*

Walkers who are intent to explore the Westend to the source must leave the track as it swings away from the river and begins to climb. The actual point is not all that clear, but keep an eye out for the faint path—it heads down towards the river bank.

The path continues as far as Grinah Grain actually on or near the banks of the river. It's a bit awkward in places, usually to get round very wet ground, but a delightful walk, with lovely pools and some interesting examples of erosion along the rocky west bank. Have a rest at the foot of Grinah Grain to admire the delightful watersmeet. If it's a hot day, you can easily go into a pleasant coma—there's a suitable bank to relax on. An interesting diversion can also be made to explore the beginning of Grinah Grain. Scramble around into the little gorge—as secret a place as you could wish for.

After the watersmeet, the driest route climbs somewhat away from the stream through bracken, before levelling out parallel to it. (it is possible to continue actually by the stream, but it is very wet). There should be no difficulty in following the path, which runs more or less on the contour above the river on the north side, as far as Deep Grain. Take a look at the "funny hump" opposite Ravens Clough where the river has obviously changed course in the past, and—if it is late summer—diverge to see the rowan trees around the small gorge just beyond the "hump". On the right day, the berries can be magnificent in colour.

Deep Grain is not easy to negotiate and does not provide a good route. Better to cross the stream, and pick your way round the eroded curve of the Westend to the next pleasant watersmeet. This is an excellent lunch spot—about an hour and a half from the car (dependent on diversions) and providing shelter from the wind in chilly weather, under the steep sides of the valley. Indeed, you will notice that by this point the open aspect of the valley has gone, and you are in a narrow V-shaped clough. The unnamed clough going somewhat south of west can be followed if your objective is The Ridge, or the Alport valley, but it is steep, wet in places, and necessitates quite a lot of jumping from bank to bank (not really difficult—it isn't very wide).

Beyond the lunchtime watersmeet, the route is lovely. Look upstream near where the small clough comes in from due north. The river (by now merely a small stream) looks exactly as though it has been landscaped by Capability Brown. The water flows down over a series of perfectly spaced waterfalls with mosses and vegetation of varying greens and browns. There are no problems in continuing actually by the water, but it is usually wet and I think the better route is to climb up the end of the spur. There is no real path, but the edge of the peat cover is soon reached and an easy route can be followed along the lip, above the stream. Cross the small stream coming in from the north and continue slightly north of west. The valley section has now been left behind and at 1,800 feet extensive views have opened out to the south and east. All around is peace and serenity; a feeling of being on the roof of England. Relax in the heather for half an hour and enjoy it.

The hillside is comparatively dry and there are no difficulties (except in mist) in choosing a route—stick to the more grassy gullies if possible. If Bleaklow Stones is the objective, stay near the more easterly of

# THE VALLEYS
## The Westend Valley, including side cloughs

the two main gullies. This leads, as it fades out into the peat groughs, to a point only just west of the Stones, on the main Bleaklow ridge, at just over 2,000 feet.

*See "Bleaklow Ridge" for ridge routes etc.*

Since you are in a valley all the way, there are no navigational difficulties, but one word of warning. Although when you wander up the valley in May, the streams may be delightful stretches of gentle water, during and after very heavy rain (with their extensive peaty headwaters) they can become raging torrents, and both the Westend itself and Deep Grain can be uncrossable. As I said in relation to Stainery Clough in the Derwent Valley, do not attempt to cross in these conditions, unless you are in a party and equipped with ropes, as it is highly dangerous. If possible stay on the same bank and proceed downstream in spite of the fact that the going may be difficult, and take your time. If this is not practicable (because of a side stream) go upstream to the point where the river may safely be crossed. Don't despair too much, as usually the small side streams are bringing in so much water that the safety point is fairly soon reached.

An extremely attractive alternative as far as Ravens Clough to the track up the valley is provided by a traverse path along the western hillside. Walk along the forest track from the gate as described earlier, as far as the bridge, but do not cross it. Walk on through the clearing, past a ruined wall to a corridor of grass between two sections of the forest. Turn left (i.e. west) up this steeply, and climb until the forest on the right ends. It's rather rough going for a bit, but follow the forest fence northwards. Soon a reasonable path is picked up at the trees running on the contour. All is very quiet here, with the forest impenetrable downwards. A little further on, the forest extends higher up the hillside, but the path continues level through the trees. Watch out for some lengths of old fencing wire lying

about (unless it's rusted away by then). The extending branches of the conifers are also rather awkward in a few places.

When the forest ends, a clear shooters' path extends along the hillside. Before the forest was planted, it must have climbed up and across the hill from the bridge, but that section is now completely obliterated. Follow this path round, admiring the extensive views across and down the valley. Do not, however, be so engrossed in the view that you trip and fall. The hillside to the right is extremely steep in some places and ends in a sheer drop into the stream bed. (This can be seen from the valley path). You wouldn't stop if you got going, and the end would be messy! After some slight ascent, the path gently descends into the bottom of Ravens Clough. (Look up that clough under the heading "Side Cloughs" if you wish to explore further). There is no path up the west bank of the Westend from here, but it is quite easy and pleasant to pick a way up as far as Deep Grain. Make sure the river is crossable if you eventually intend to do that.

## THE SIDE CLOUGHS

All the significant cloughs except one are on the western side of the valley, and whilst some of these provide useful routes to the tops, in many cases there are no legal access.

## RIDGE CLOUGH

This is the exception and it rises not from the actual valley but from the road half-way along the Westend arm of the reservoir. It is a short clough rising steeply to reach 1,500 feet quickly, but it is delightful in shape and in quietness. There is, however, no legal access.

# THE VALLEYS
## The Westend Valley, including side cloughs

## DITCH AND GREEN CLOUGHS

Not many yards from the road through the
Westend forest gate, the waters of Ditch
and Green Clough flow under the track
into the Westend River. For an exploration
of these cloughs, turn left before the
crossing and wander upstream through the
forest trees, more or less alongside the
water. In quite a short distance a wall—the
edge of the forest—is reached. The area
here is sylvan and delightful—so near the
road and so different. The lower section of
Green Clough can be explored with
pleasure but the complete ascent is not
very rewarding and it leads only to the
subsidiary top of Birchinlee, with a very
heathery climb to the main ridge, or a
difficult descent into Ouzelden. Ditch
Clough is well named, being narrow,
deeply incised and almost straight. When
the water is not high, it provides a
scrambly climb up to the top and out not
far from Alport Castles. It is an alternative
to the normal one up the path (see
Westend Valley) but it is inferior to it, since
there are no views.

## FAGNEY CLOUGH

Fagney Clough leaves the main river less
than half a mile from the forest gate at the
site of the long-disappeared Westend
Farm. At the moment there is a small
wooden forestry hut situated there. The
clough looks attractive on the map—a
good way up to the ridge—but it isn't. The
sides are very steep, there is no path and
the climb at the end is somewhat
wearisome. In any case there is no access.

## RAVENS CLOUGH

This is a treeless, rocky and secret clough,
leaving the valley about half-way up. There
is a shooters' path up the northern side,
but once again there is no legal access.

## BLACK CLOUGH

A heavily forested valley and again no
legal access.

# THE TOPS

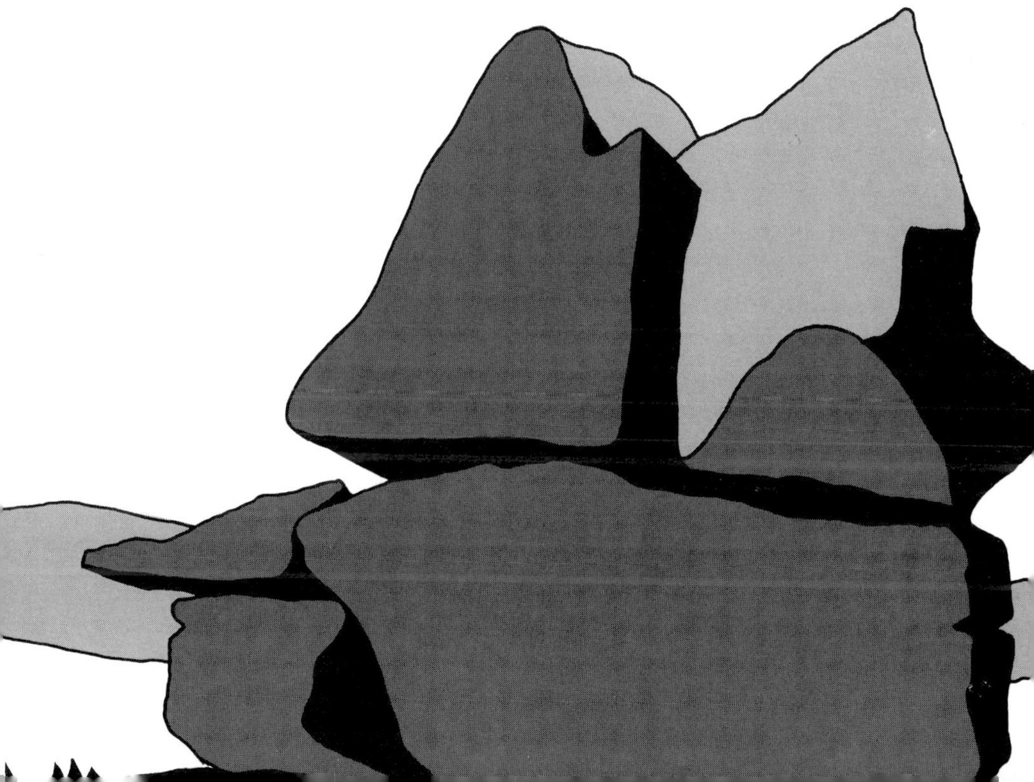

# CHAPTER 5

## GENERAL COMMENTS

Almost all the high ground in the area covered by this book is open country. Part of it is owned by the National Trust and for the rest there are access agreements, so that the walker—provided he conforms to the by-laws—can walk from anywhere to anywhere by any feasible route, without let or hindrance. He can ignore all paths and all suggested routes and pick his way over the tops via the cloughs and ridges which take his fancy. The routes which are suggested here are the easier ways up (or down) and are those which I have found most rewarding, but the fact that my dotted line goes up one gully does not mean you have to go up that one. The next one two hundred yards away may be just as good.

Before the mid-1950's the Bleaklow area was strictly private. There were no paths at all, except the shooters' routes up from the valleys, and a faint path up the Alport as far as Grains-in-the-Water, which was—and is—used by shepherds. Even the Eastern Edges were crossed by only three public paths—Moscar-Derwent, Strines-Abbey Bank and Flouch-Slippery Stones (Cut Gate). Gradually, however, trodden ways have developed, usually between groups of rocks (obvious landmarks in a featureless landscape) or along the ridges. Even in 1970 most of these were only faint trails through the heather, but now in some cases are real walkers' thoroughfares. When I use the clear path from Grinah to Bleaklow Stones, I often think, almost with disbelief, that in 1960 it didn't exist and the walker just picked a way round.

Since the paths which have developed were not planned and did not begin specifically leading from point A to point B as they did in the limestone area—from village to leadmine—they are sometimes rather deceptive to the stranger. There can be a perfectly reasonable path leading away from a group of rocks for about two hundred yards but which then disappears. Or along a ridge, the path can disappear as it crosses a depression where the groughs make the going more difficult and each walker chooses his own route. This can be disconcerting especially in mist, and the walker would do well to remember these facts, and not entirely trust the path to lead to safety, or indeed to anywhere.

Despite the reputation the Bleaklow area seems to have (mainly, I feel, because of the over-used Pennine Way—see my comments under "The Bleaklow Ridge") the going is generally quite reasonable for the hill walker, though people in flimsy shoes would find it difficult and should not attempt it. There are fewer landmarks by which to navigate than on Kinder, for instance, so be sure of your navigational skills, and go warm and well-equipped.

Like all of highland Britain, the ground is often wet—even on the ridges—but, apart from the direct route from Wain Stones to Bleaklow Stones, i.e. along the ridge itself, there are almost none of the deep peat groughs of the Kinder Plateau type which make walking progress so difficult. Real bogs are few and far between (do not confuse soggy wet ground with bog) and they can always be avoided. The worst walking, I think, is over areas of tussocky grass and through deep heather—avoid these if possible; if not possible, grit your teeth and push on—a useful exercise in determination. A little basic knowledge of botany can be useful in choosing the best and driest route. Heather, for example, will not grow in very wet ground, whereas bright green moss indicates bog. Avoid crossing the splayed out gullies at the head of most of the side cloughs (a good example is Stainery). It is always better to go round the watershed, even if it's a bit further.

The great thing about the area is its openness and freedom. No need to bother about stiles and farms and rights of way. Here the adventurous walker can let himself go, striking out over the hills with a sense of exploration in a miniature wilderness, and ending the day with a real feeling of satisfaction and achievement.

# CHAPTER 6

# THE TOPS EASTERN EDGES

# DERWENT EDGE, ASHOPTON TO BACK TOR

Derwent Edge begins from Ashopton (or what is left of it) in a fairly sharp nose—for the Peak District—and runs north for about three miles to Back Tor. North of there, the edge is cut by the deep valley of Abbey Brook. It is clearly visible for almost all of its length from the motor road running north on the arm of the Ladybower Reservoir. I can never imagine anyone with spirit on that road, looking up at the intriguing rocks and tors along the eastern horizon without wishing desperately to climb up and explore them. The views along the entire length are good and the going comparatively easy. In addition, in common with most ridges and edges, once the height is gained there is little more climbing to be done. One word of warning; if there is a very strong wind from a westerly direction (the prevailing direction) it may be as well to postpone the expedition. The air forced upwards by the steep hillside when added to that blowing across, can produce wind strengths of remarkable proportions, making walking hard work and difficult. A limited number of cars may be parked in the lay-by just east of Ashopton Viaduct, by the telephone box. This is part of suggested walks Nos. 1, 2 and 3.

Two routes are recommended from Ashopton—one steep and abrupt (with superb views), the other longer but very much easier. Both start up the track

# DERWENT EDGE
## ASHOPTON TO BACK TOP
## Map 12

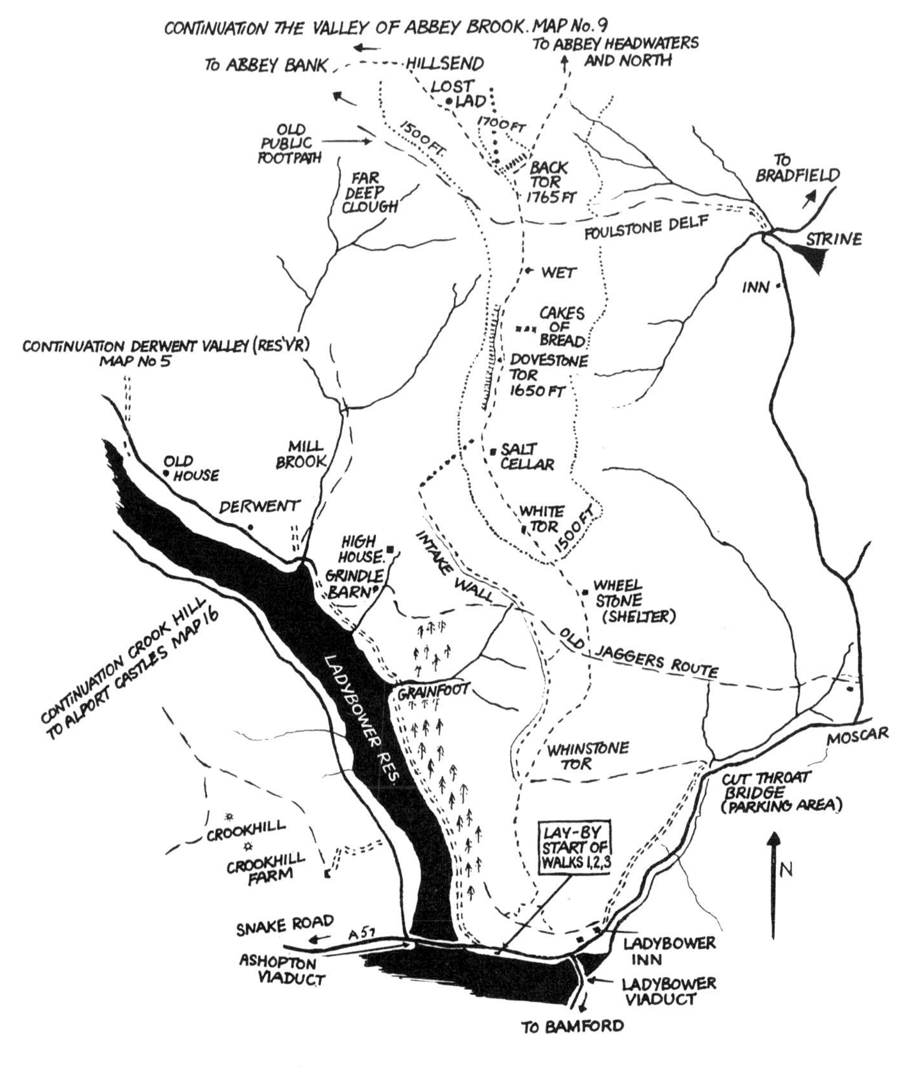

alongside the Ladybower Inn on the east side. I'll take the steep one first. Within yards of leaving the main road, a clear path doubles back off the track round the rear of the inn and, almost immediately, the rear of a large house. After passing through a gate, the path continues alongside a wall. Keep to the path up the steep hillside, pausing at intervals to look at the bird's eye view of the Ladybower Reservoir below. A more obvious and continuous path is soon picked up which runs up and along the edge with the ground falling away to the left, giving lovely views of the valley and this can be followed without difficulty to Whinstone Lee Tor. Just short of the tor, there is a V-shaped break in the rocks on the left and this point is a bit of a junction. A route comes in from Cut-Throat Bridge (see below) and a route goes left between the rocks, to join the intake wall.

To reach that point the easy way (and it is so gradual you are scarcely aware of any climbing, except at first—highly recommended to active grandmothers) continue along the track from the inn. It runs pleasantly through trees (part of the Derbyshire Naturalists' Trust Ladybower Wood Nature Reserve), then bracken and heather and although it is parallel to and not far from the main road, it is quiet. Towards Cut-Throat Bridge, it dips and joins the path coming up from the road by the side of a pretty moorland stream. Notices announce (or did) that the way ahead is private, but worry not—turn to take the path running due west. There is no further difficulty. It climbs very, very gently across the heathery hillside, with lovely views of Win Hill to the south, to join the direct path as indicated.

A reasonably clear path climbs past Whinstone Lee Tor and up the edge, eventually crossing at right angles the old public footpath. This is part of the old Jaggers route and gives easy access to the edge from the reservoir track near Derwent or from the east near Moscar. After this crossing, Wheel Stones are clearly visible ahead. These well-named stones are worth an examination as they present a remarkable example of gritstone weathering—they also provide good shelter for a short rest. The path ahead is quite easy to follow, indeed it is becoming so well used that in places it has become braided, but all the branches lead along the edge. White Tor is a good viewpoint and the aptly named "Cakes o' Bread" lie to the east. If you have enough time, linger a little at Dovestone Tor and have a look at the impressive crag under the edge. Few people bother to do so, and it's worth a look. The section of the path from Dovestone to the Strines—Abbey path is usually rather wet, but diversions over drier patches can help. The Strines-Abbey path is signposted, and if you want to reduce the walk, you can turn here— whichever way is suitable for your return. Most people, however, will choose to go on to the logical end of the edge at Back Tor.

Back Tor is a large and impressive group of rocks, with an abrupt face to the north, tailing away to the east. It is a good place for lunch, offering adequate shelter but, as there is too much foreground at almost the same height, the view is rather disappointing. If this is an important object of the exercise, it is better to go on to Lost Lad, where the view is superb. To get there is quite simple. Turn north west from the western end of the rocks, down a small dip, and follow the clear path (though rather wet) over a minor hill, across a depression and up to the trig point. It can be very exposed—there is no shelter—but may I repeat, the view is highly recommended.

Routes for Back Tor are:

1.  **East of north on the peaty path from the eastern end of the rocks.**

2.  **Due north into Sheepfold Clough (rough).**

3.  **North west, as indicated, for Lost Lad, Hillsend and Abbey Bank.**

*(See Abbey Valley for details).*

# EASTERN EDGES
## HOWDEN EDGE TO SWAINS HEAD
### Map 13

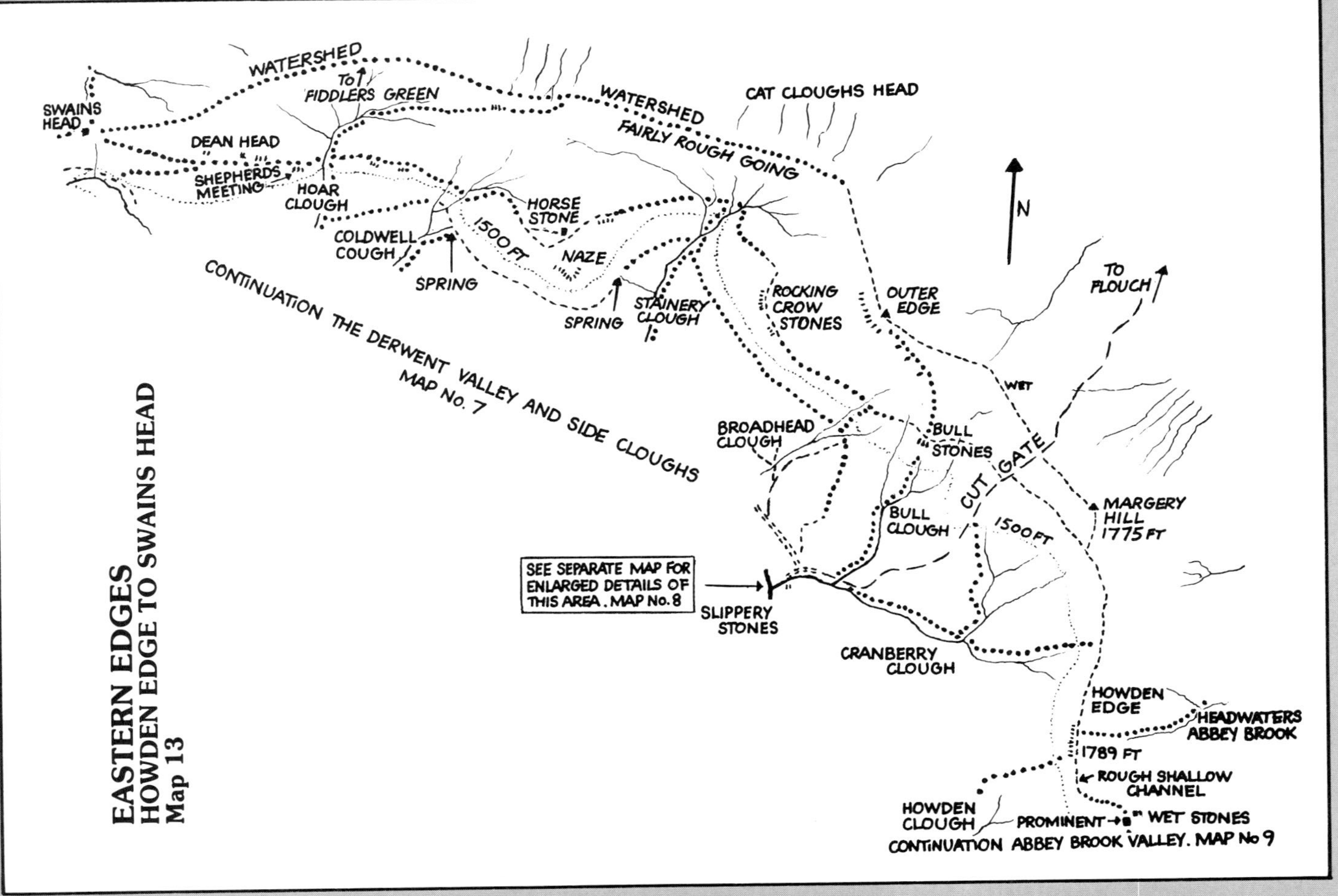

# CHAPTER 7

# THE TOPS EASTERN EDGES

# HOWDEN EDGE, MARGERY HILL, HORSE STONE, OUTER EDGE, SHEPHERDS' MEETING STONES

Routes to Howden Edge-High Stones will normally be from somewhere in Abbey Brook or Howden Clough—and details are given under the Howden or Abbey Brook Valley chapter.

The section north to the Cut Gate path is, I think, the best "edge" walk in the Peak Park. The going is easy (unless a westerly gale is blowing) and dry; the views are spectacular covering the Upper Derwent, the Bleaklow ridge and way across to Kinder; and the feeling is one of airy openness. It is exhilarating. There is a beautiful view down Cranberry Clough, and the huge moorland bowl below is empty and silent. A diversion from the edge path is needed to reach Margery Hill (scarcely any climbing) but I always think the peaty hump is not very rewarding. The Cut Gate path is very clear (you can't over-run it even in mist) and it offers very safe routes down, easterly to the Flouch Inn (a pleasant enough path, but peaty, especially to begin with) or westerly to Slippery Stones and the Packhorse Bridge. This latter has attractive views all the way and presents no difficulties.

*There are two suggested routes north from the Cut Gate path. The first is via Outer Edge and round Stainery Clough Head, and the second via Bull Stones, Crow Stones and Horse Stone.*

# THE TOPS
## Eastern Edges – Howden Edge to Shepherd's Meeting Stones

Via Outer Edge. This is a route I enjoy least of all those described in this book. It is generally wet, rough and featureless. After the pleasures of Howden Edge, it is an anticlimax to tackle the very wet section across the flat moor top to Outer Edge. A faint path leaves Cut Gate just east of the summit, but it is not very easy to find and is of doubtful assistance when found. Many diversions are needed to avoid really wet areas (unless the weather has been exceptionally dry) and one can only be pleased to start on the more heathery climb up to Outer Edge. This is the best point on the route and the rocks to the west of the trig point provide a pleasant place to rest. The path continues almost due north for half a mile, past an old boundary stone. The best point at which to turn north west round Stainery Clough Head is debatable and opinions may vary. (Incidentally, don't be tempted to cut across from Outer Edge—the groughs of Stainery Clough Head are awful). I find the best place is just before the heather becomes more predominant. Wherever you do it, the going is now rough and you can only slog on up the slightly rising ground. There is a faint and intermittent path if you can find it, and this becomes somewhat clearer towards the top—east of Ruck Hoar Stone.

If you are intent to go round the Derwent headquarters, and are not exhausted, continue somewhat west of north west, keeping to the higher ground round Hoar Clough Head and turning west to Swains Head. I am sorry no clearer guide can be given, but the moor is featureless and you can only pick your way. If you wish to get down to the valley, leave the higher ground a little to the north west of Ruck Hoar Stone and—losing height gently—follow the south side of the long east-west channel leading towards Hoar Clough. Descend into the stream bed at the point where several channels meet, and follow it to the edge, where the stream drops sharply. A path leads round on the edge to Shepherds' Meeting Stones not far away. This is a fine, lonely spot, with a view down the valley and across to Barrow Stones. The rocks are so named because, many, many years ago, they provided a central meeting point for shepherds from the Derwent Valley on the one side and the Langsett area on the other. The shepherds met here to gather in all the sheep before sorting them in the sheep pens below.

From Shepherds' Meeting Stones, or the head of Hoar Clough, several routes are possible. If you are aiming for Fiddlers Green, the way is somewhat east of north and the going rather rough. An easy descent south will take you down to the Derwent Valley, either to return or to climb up to Barrow Stones. If you are going round the headwaters, walk across the hillside, west, climbing slightly to Dean Head Stones, then to Swains Head.

Via Horse Stone. Back to Cut Gate and the second route. It must be mentioned at the outset, that the going via Crow Stones and Horse Stone is rough practically all the way. There is, in places, a bit of a path, but for much of the distance it is a question of making your way through the heather. Having said that, the route is much more rewarding than via Outer Edge. Since you are on the edge all the way, the views down into the changing valley are pleasant and the rock outcrops provide interest. A faint path leaves Cut Gate a little way below the top, just under the lip and runs erratically north, then north west, round the head of Bull Clough, to Bull Stones. This is an impressive group of rocks, jutting out from the hillside. The views are very good, and there is convenient shelter. (You can, from here, join the previously described route at Outer Edge by walking north up the hillside).Keep to the edge, however, for Crow Stones and take the faint path at the back of the rocks. This path soon fades out and though from time to time advantage can be taken of a more distinct route, it is largely a question of picking a way through fairly deep heather.

You will find it best to keep on the lip, just above where the ground falls away more steeply, but this can only be a rough guide. You should cross a gully above Broadhead Clough which contains the remains of a light aircraft which plunged into the hillside long ago. Most of the smaller remains have disappeared in the peat or have been taken away (illegally!) by the strange breed of souvenir hunters, but the engine and odd bits lie sadly in the peat. Please note that digging and/or the removal of souvenirs is forbidden except with the express authority of both the landowner and the Ministry of Defence. Head for the rocks visible ahead and from there, an easy level path runs along to Crow and Rocking Stones.

This is a superb viewpoint and well worth making the object of an easy day's expedition. The rocks themselves are imposing, carved by the weather over millions of years into strange shapes. Rocking Stone, at the north end is a remarkable piece of rock, and balanced in a most unlikely fashion. It can be seen at its best from further down the hillside towards the waterfall at the head of Stainery Clough. The view covers a wide sweep from Holme Moss across Bleaklow to Kinder and the lower hills to the south, but the dominant feature is the beautiful sight of the waters of the Howden and Derwent Reservoirs stretching away down the valley two or three miles away. This is a place to linger at on a warm day—try to make it the lunch or tea break. See Map No. 14 for sky-line view. Try to identify them all.

A clear path leads off from the north end of the rocks, slightly down-hill to a group of small rocks. The path here turns left (north) but quickly disappears. Continue down the gently sloping hillside as though heading for the clough, but swing to the right about two hundred yards from it into deeper heather, where a peaty path of

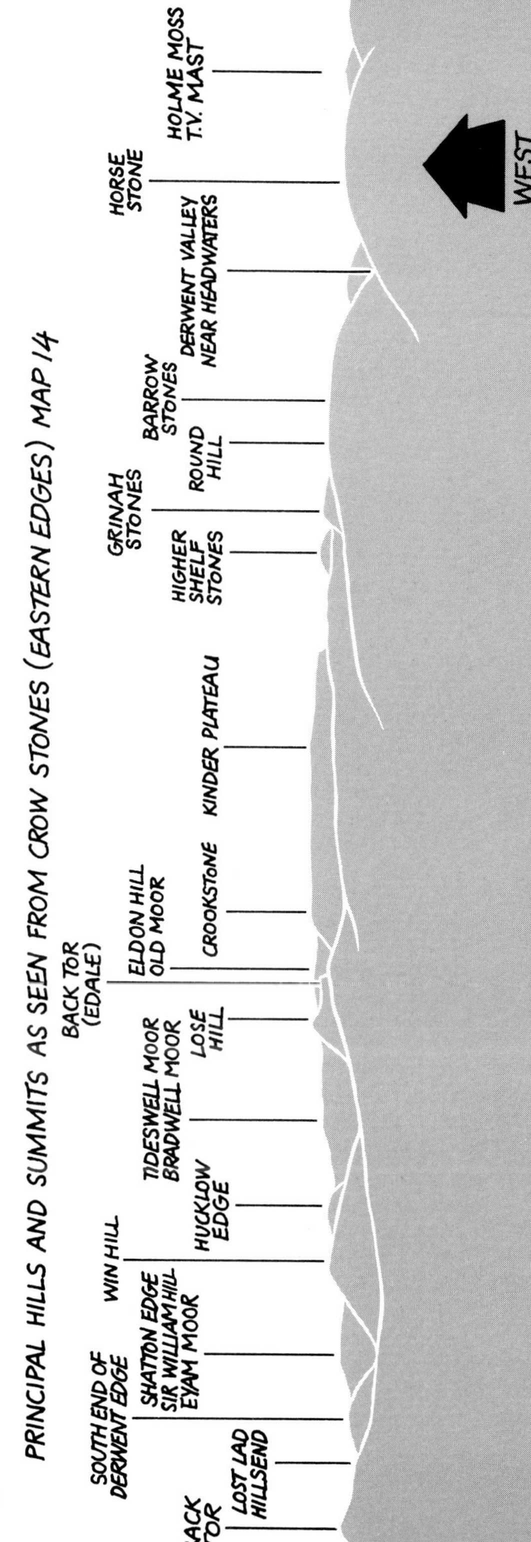

sorts will be found leading to the waterfall at the top of Stainery Clough proper. The many peat channels of Stainery Clough Head splay out from here.

The next objective is Horse Stone, but there is only small help to be obtained from a very intermittent path. There are two small side cloughs to be crossed (no difficulty) and a rather awkward channel of bog. This can be crossed in one or two places, but if you are unhappy about it, move a little down the hillside to the point where the bright green moss ends in a small stream and cross there. The climb up the hillside (almost due west) as far as the more prominent rocks a little short of Horse Stone, should be done gently—it is not a hillside to rush up. There is no real path and the best advice—and this can only be general—is to keep to the higher line of low rocks. Once the more prominent rocks are reached (from which there is a lovely view south) the difficulties are temporarily over as a reasonable path leads to Horse Stone and beyond.

Horse Stone itself is disappointing, just a chunk of gritstone on the flat moor top, but the Naze to the west is worth a little exploration if you're interested in rock scenery. The route now turns north, and though the faint path continues for a time it soon fades away—near to a solitary stake (if it's still there). No way across Coldwell Clough Head is particularly easy, but it is best to turn a little right over more grassy ground, and eventually pick up a long peat channel. Follow this down a bit to an area where several channels link, and strike out for the rocks to the north over ground denuded of vegetation—a peat desert. From the first rocks, it is comparatively easy to pick a way along the edge to Hoar Clough.

On days when the tops are in mist, or when you're feeling lazy, there's a worthwhile traverse path from Broadhead Clough to Coldwell. Climb about half way up Broadhead (in height) on the shooters'

path and then move left along the hillside on a sheep path. One of these—and you may have to cast about a bit to find it—at about 1,400 feet continues through bracken and heather, almost into Stainery Clough. Cross the stream at the point where there is a more than usual amount of rock, and continue, swinging westwards, at about the same height. After a bit of rough ground, a path can be picked up just about at Horse Stone spring, and followed round and below Horse Stone Naze and then north west across the hillside to Coldwell Spring. This route can, of course, be followed in the opposite direction and makes a pleasant leisurely end to a day—though of course you forfeit the long-distance views.

# CHAPTER 8

# THE TOPS

# RONKSLEY MOOR RIDGE

The ridge of Ronksley Moor, stretching from Round Hill to Ridge Clough, is central to several exciting walks. It is likely to be used in part outward or return on any route round the Westend Headwaters via Bleaklow Stones from the Westend forest gate. It will almost certainly be used from the King's Tree for walks round or to the Derwent headwaters via Barrow Stones. Fortunately it is a comparatively easy ridge, reasonably good going, with a defined route for most of the way which can be followed, even in mist. The views are good throughout, sweeping from the line of Kinder in the west, south past Lose Hill, Win Hill to the long Eastern Edge running in a continuous line in the east. rocks of Bleaklow Stones, Grinah and Climbing, the Barrow beckon on the moorland skyline.

The great thing about Ronksley from a navigational point of view is the wide shallow channel in the peat cover running from a point above Linch Clough, with only a small change in direction, to the "crossroads" where the shooters' track from the Westend meets the route up from Lower Small Clough. As will be seen from reference to the detailed sketch map headed "Ronksley Moor Ridge", all routes up from the valleys join this this channel somewhere. From the King's Tree, one of the routes detailed in the chapter describing Linch Clough will probably be used. From the Westend, either Ridge Clough, or one of the steep climbs up the hillside from the valley will be best. By far the easiest and, in mist, the safest route is up the Westend shooters' track which leads on to the top of the ridge at the northern end of the wide channel, and which leaves no great distance to walk to Barrow or Grinah.

The channel starts over the lip of the steep hillside of Linch Clough and after running south west for a short distance turns 90 degree and runs north west almost straight, up to a large shooting butt. It is a gentle, easy climb, with a faint path over the coarse grass and no possiblilty of going astray.

# THE TOPS
## Ronksley Moor Ridge

There is a line of shooting butts on the right over the last section. The channel opens out somewhat and here the routes up from the Westend, and from Linch Clough itself (see "Side Cloughs") join. There is a slight change of direction (northerly) and after about one hundred yards another wide channel appears from the direction of the Linch Clough headquarters. It is possible to walk in this channel, but the going is better by the path which has developed on the west side of it. There is little alteration in height to the "crossroads".

Your position here is identifiable even in poor visibility. A deep, narrow and straight channel runs away north east, providing a sure route to Lower Small Clough and the Derwent Valley. Exactly opposite, another peat gully leads within yards to the top of the shooters' track.

The way forward lies up the peat bank to the left of the deep Lower Small Clough gully and a reasonable, though wet, path continues north north-west. If you are bound for Round Hill and Barrow Stones, watch for a faint path which goes off to the right due north to the foot of the steeper slope. The dry, steepish climb to Round Hill is easily done—pause at the top for the good view of the Upper Derwent—and then, turning almost 90 degrees to north west, head across the slight depression towards the Crown Stone and Barrow Stones. The faint path crosses Grinah Grain almost at the head over a peat gully becoming more slimy each year, and up the dry heathery hillside direct to the Crown Stone.

If you are making for Grinah, continue on the path, which loses some height into Grinah Grain. A path proceeds through the heather directly over the stream, but loses itself in the wetter ground ahead. It is better not to head straight for the rocks, but to pick a way directly up the hillside to where a line of grass slopes up and across the hillside. From then on choose one of the grassy gullies and come up under the stones themselves.

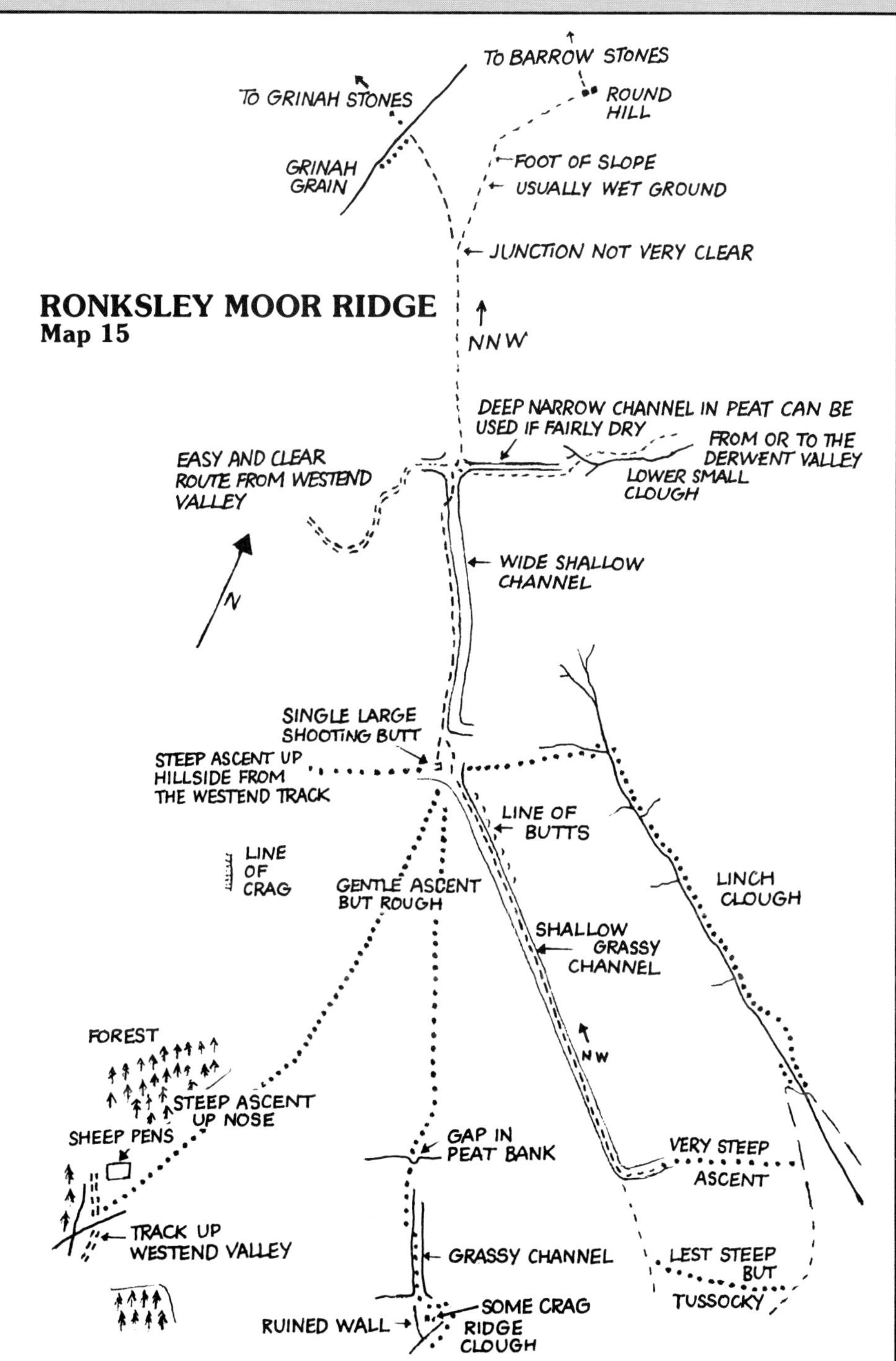

TO BARROW STONES
TO GRINAH STONES
ROUND HILL
GRINAH GRAIN
FOOT OF SLOPE
USUALLY WET GROUND
JUNCTION NOT VERY CLEAR
RONKSLEY MOOR RIDGE
Map 15
NNW
DEEP NARROW CHANNEL IN PEAT CAN BE USED IF FAIRLY DRY
FROM OR TO THE DERWENT VALLEY
LOWER SMALL CLOUGH
EASY AND CLEAR ROUTE FROM WESTEND VALLEY
WIDE SHALLOW CHANNEL
N
SINGLE LARGE SHOOTING BUTT
STEEP ASCENT UP HILLSIDE FROM THE WESTEND TRACK
LINE OF BUTTS
LINE OF CRAG
GENTLE ASCENT BUT ROUGH
LINCH CLOUGH
SHALLOW GRASSY CHANNEL
NW
FOREST
STEEP ASCENT UP NOSE
SHEEP PENS
GAP IN PEAT BANK
VERY STEEP ASCENT
TRACK UP WESTEND VALLEY
GRASSY CHANNEL
LEST STEEP BUT TUSSOCKY
SOME CRAG
RUINED WALL
RIDGE CLOUGH

# CROOK HILL TO ALPORT CASTLES
## Map 16

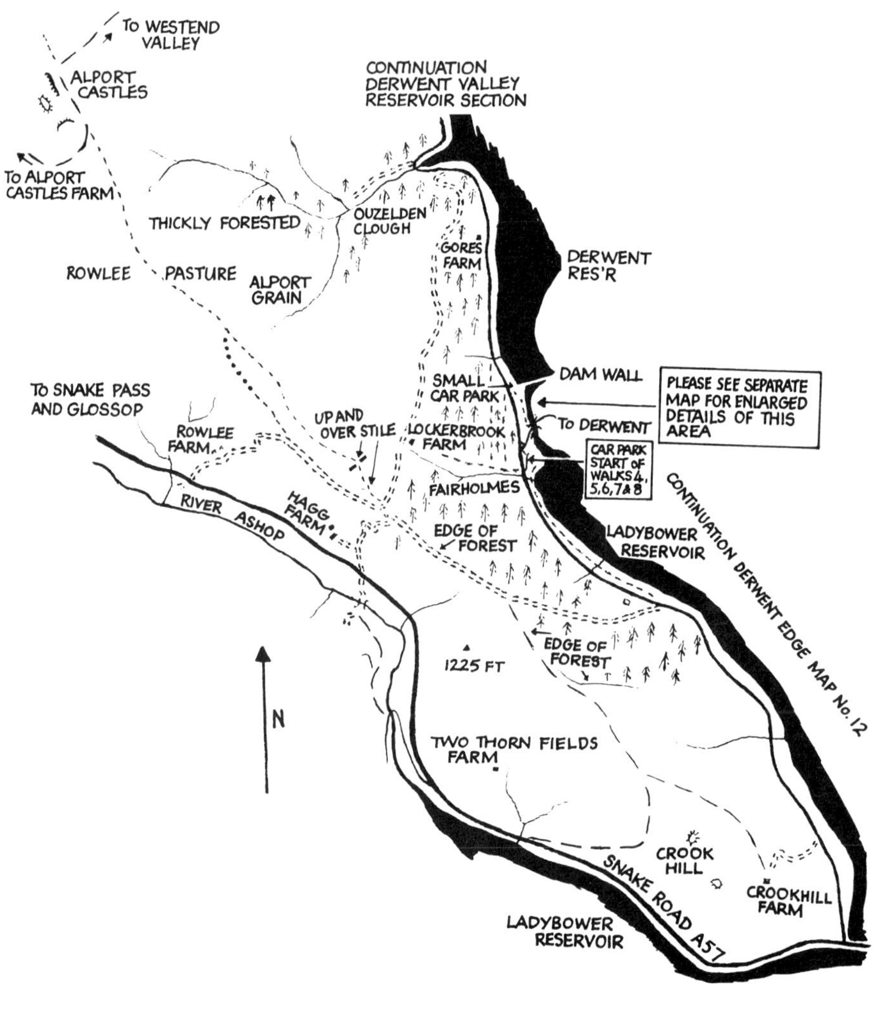

# CHAPTER 9

# THE TOPS

# CROOK HILL TO ALPORT CASTLES

This section is really a continuation of the long ridge which comes down from Bleaklow between the valleys of the Westend and the Alport. It is much less wild and much nearer civilisation than the Alport Castles to Bleaklow section, and furthermore is is crossed by several clear tracks. Nevertheless, it is an attractive area with lovely views over the valleys and provides good walking not only as an approach to the higher ground, but for people who like a more gentle walk without the rough going and real desolation.

The bridle path via Crookhill Farm leaving the Derwent road a little way north of the Ashopton Viaduct, though quite straight forward, has one disadvantage I think. Unless you are fortunate enough to have someone to drop you and take the car on to, say, the Westend gate or Alport Castles farm, a circle is difficult to arrange without a considerable mileage of walking on a motor road (during the summer you can of course catch the minibus which runs up and down the valley road on summer Sundays and Bank Holidays). Inevitably you will descend to the Derwent Valley Road or the Snake Road. You can avoid the road walk only by descending and crossing the Derwent Valley under the dam, returning along the east track. If you dislike this type of walking as much as I

do, the route will be of little use. However, there are no problems. After the farm, the path turns and passes below the two rocky humps of Crook Hill, thence climbing gradually to 1,275 feet in a north westerly direction, with excellent views all round. After a slight descent, the edge of the forest appears on the right and continues alongside for nearly a mile. Where the fence slightly changes direction (by a gate) the bridle path up from the Derwent Valley road joins. This latter is a pleasant alternative forest walk from the valley, with a convenient car park only yards away from the start. The path continues level to the main junction above Hagg Farm. All this route follows public rights of way but the land adjacent is private.

At this point, two other possible upward routes join.

**(a) From the Derwent Valley road near Ouzelden Clough. This track is pleasant enough and quiet (note the lovely view north towards the Howden Reservoir from Wrenhey Coppice) but the views east towards Derwent Edge, which would be delightful, are cut off for almost the entire way by the thick forest. What a wonderful place to live Lockerbrook Farm must have been, with that superb view down the valley. The buildings are now repaired and in good order and the place is used — but not as a farm.**

**(b) From the Snake Road to the south, the old Jaggers route from Edale and beyond zig-zags up the hillside through the trees, past the end of the Hagg Farm drive. Hagg Farm is now owned by the Peak National Park Authority, the farm building being lived in by the Area Ranger in the Eastern District, and the renovated out-buildings in use as a splendid youth hostel. (Open to non-YHA members) with an adjacent "light-weight" camp site.**

# THE TOPS
## Crook Hill to Alport Castles

The logical way forward for Alport Castles is up the ridge, north west from the junction of tracks. Follow the concessionary path up to the first up-and-over stile, clearly visible ahead (an excellent viewpoint looking south), and then up the right hand side of the wall to the second stile. This is the access point to open country. The path—almost a track at first—swings somewhat to the left before climbing gently up the ridge, almost exactly north west.

The views are superb throughout—west to the Ashop Valley and Kinder; east to the long line of the Eastern Edges. The path over Rowlee Pasture becomes very wet, and as it decends slightly, a change of direction to north north-west is needed. Once across the depression between Ouzeldene Clough and the Alport Valley, the edge of the shattered cliffs of Alport Castles is soon reached.

*Alport Castles*

# THE TOPS

# ALPORT CASTLES TO BLEAKLOW RIDGE

Alport Castles will almost certainly have been reached by one of three easy routes:

**(a) From the Westend Forest gate (see "The Westend Valley" chapter for details); or**

**(b) From Alport Castles Farm (where there is a Peak National Park Camping Barn), crossing the Alport river by the bridge east of the farm and up the clear public footpath to the southern end of the rocks; or**

**(c) From the Snake Road via the flattish ridge south east of the Castles, called Rowlee Pasture — though there's precious little pasture, (see "Crook Hill to Alport Castles" for details).**

**It is quite an impressive spot especially later on a clear sunny day, when Kinder to the west is etched against the brilliant light, and hills to the south are in sunlight.**

The most dramatic approach is from the Westend, since from this direction the view opens up suddenly as the top is reached, with the yawning chasm across to the "Castles" abruptly cutting the forward line of the path. This is said to be the largest landslip in the country and it's certainly big, with a lot of crag and tumbled rock. This area is very dangerous for any climbing or scrambling, and is protected as a Site of Special Scientific Interest (SSSI), so please give it the respect it deserves.

There is no difficulty in finding the path for the ridge. It starts some yards short of the drop, exactly parallel to the wall running north west, on the easterly side. I always think that on this start more perhaps than anywhere else, you have the feeling of a departure for the wilderness. Behind are the green fields of the Alport Valley, with odd farms and even a good road; ahead is a largely trackless waste as far as you can see, to the distant ridge. An exciting

# THE TOPS
## Alport Castles to Bleaklow Ridge

prospect—for some! The path continues on the very edge of the moor for about three-quarters of a mile until you dip (slightly) in and out of two side streams. As you climb out of the second and larger stream bed, turn north away from the edge, skirting some very wet ground for a short way. (note that it is possible to continue on the lip of the moor—no path—across Glethering Clough, to join the main Alport Valley path in Miry Clough, but this involves loss of height). A faint path can be picked up, which turns north west (if you can't find it, turn north west anyway) and continues over what is usually fairly wet ground to the Trig point. This is a good view point, but affords no shelter, so—except on hot days—your stay will probably be short. Just after the Trig point a short detour is necessary to avoid some watery peat pools, but the path is traceable losing a little height into the depression between Miry and Glethering Cloughs to the west, and Black and Ravens Cloughs to the east.

This is an area of peat groughs (the headwaters of the four cloughs mentioned) and any clear path disappears, so that it is necessary to pick our way by the driest route possible, until the ground rises again. The direction remains the same—north-west. Though drier, the going over the higher ground (1,750 feet) is rough and this continues over the next depression. As the ground begins to rise again towards the ridge marked on the O.S. map as "The Ridge" at 1,819 feet, a change of direction to north is necessary. There is a faint path running through the peaty patches on top and another one across the coarse grass immediately to the west. These paths continue, swinging somewhat east, into the headwaters of the Westend. The more easterly of the main gullies (there are others) will take you up to the main Bleaklow Ridge, a little to the west of Bleaklow Stones. Alternatively, it is quite easy to head more directly up and across the hillside to the Stones.

*Upper Alport in winter*

# ALPORT CASTLES TO BLEAKLOW RIDGE
## THE ALPORT VALLEY INCLUDING ASCENTS FROM THE SNAKE ROAD
**Map 17**

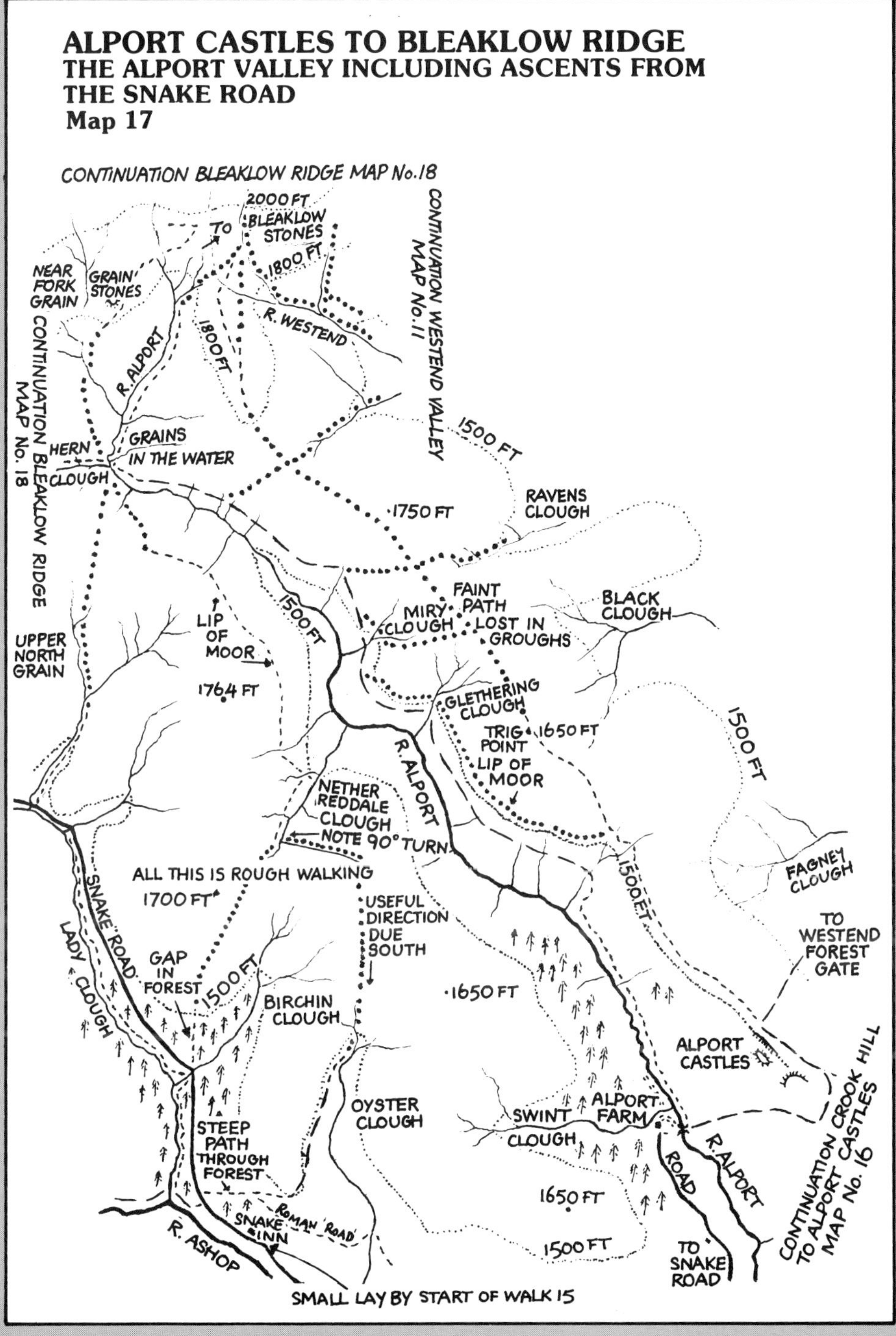

# CHAPTER 11

# THE TOPS

# THE ALPORT VALLEY TO GRAINS IN THE WATER

# INCLUDING ASCENTS FROM THE SNAKE ROAD

It is interesting to speculate why this valley, being only a few miles from the Westend and the Derwent, with the same rock and similar streams, is not more like them. It should be—but it is not. Both the Westend and Derwent are comparatively wide until near the headwaters, whereas the Alport for most of its length is steeply V-shaped, almost indeed a gorge, with the lip of the moors high above the stream. Though perhaps lacking the gentler charm of its neighbours, the Alport is nevertheless impressive, wild and well-worth exploration. Since the valley is so narrow, there are no long side cloughs, though Nether Reddale Clough is useful, when crossing to or from the Snake Inn.

There is no legal right of way up the Alport Valley, and no access agreements exist until you reach the area above Miry Clough. However, at some future date it is the intention to formalise a right of way.

Usually in wild country, a path starts clearly but deteriorates or disappears further on. In this case, however, the least distinct part (as far as Grains-in-the-Water) is the first section. Unless the river is low—when you cross it higher up—it is best to use the bridge to the east of Alport Castles Farm, as though going up the hillside to the Castles. Turn and follow the stream northwards, using the faint paths, often through bracken, as far as the first major stream from the eastern side. If you climb about half way up the hillside, you will pick up a clear path running up-valley parallel to the river. Thirty years ago—or even fifteen—this was a faint shepherds' path leading into the hills, but has now become well-established and indeed shows signs of walkers' erosion in places, but on a minor scale. Once having found it, there are no further navigational difficulties, as it leads unerringly to Grains-in-the-Water.

Since the path runs high up the hillside, the views down to the stream are excellent and the stream is a delight all the way. Have a look if you've time (and don't mind losing the height) at the gorge with waterfalls just before Miry Clough and at the beautiful waterfall just north of Miry Clough. Incidentally, there is some loss of height and a subsequent climb in crossing Miry, but nothing serious. In places the hillside is so steep around here as to produce several lines of crag on both sides of the river—don't fall over them. After the path crosses the 1,500 feet contour, the valley becomes noticeably shallower but frequent halts are still recommended to peer at the stream bed especially the half-mile before Grains-in-the-Water. There are waterfalls, water-slides, glorious pools and a lovely stretch on bed rock.

◀ *Grains in the Water*

# THE TOPS
## The Alport Valley to Grains in the Water

The watersmeet at Grains-in-the-Water is a wild yet infinitely peaceful spot in the wide bowl of the hills. It has the feeling of being in the middle of it all. I have often seen it with all the streams frozen solid and a bank of snow 10 feet deep piled on the east side, but perhaps it is best on a warm day in summer when the only sound is the murmuring of the water, and the shrill world of people and cities seems a million miles away.

The route from here depends on your objective. If for Higher Shelf or Wain Stones or a traverse along Bleaklow Ridge, follow the faint path on the north side of Hern Clough. After a short way it moves up the hillside, away from the stream somewhat, before going back to the stream bed at the junction with the Pennine Way. If for Grains Stones or Bleaklow Stones, follow the intermittent path on the east side of the stream up to Alport Head. (Please see Bleaklow Ridge chapter for various routes).

An alternative to the route up the valley given above, but only for the strong and adventurous, is to make your way upstream in or alongside the stream bed. It is awkward in places, especially around the gorge, and involves some jumping and scrambling, but is good fun—if you're that way inclined!

*Upper Alport*

# THE TOPS
## The Alport Valley to Grains in the Water

The Alport Valley described in these pages is the one in which the (then) Rover Scouts perished in the early sixties, having been despatched incredibly ill-equipped for a high-level walk in March, which can still be vicious winter on this high ground. Two of the bodies were found near the waterfall, half a mile north of Miry Clough. This tragic incident led directly to the formation of the Peak District Mountain Rescue Organisation, which co-ordinates the work of the individual rescue teams. Their valuable service is often—too often—called upon and since it is purely voluntary, donations are always very welcome.

May I use this as a reminder that all this area of high moorland can be very dangerous—especially from early November to April (and sometimes outside even these dates). Walkers should, therefore, in there own interest, ensure that their equipment and behaviour is in accordance with the rules of Mountain Safety.

## CROSSING TO THE ALPORT FROM THE SNAKE ROAD

The stretch of moorland ridge from Over Wood Moss to Cowms Rocks can only be recommended, I think, to the energetic—the walkers who like striding over a pathless ocean of heather and coarse grass. The views are good but the going is rough.

There is, however, a very-worth-while route on the lip of the moor up the west side of the Alport, which can be reached from the Snake Road, suggested walk No. 15. The best route across is via Oyster Clough. The path leaves the Snake Road about a quarter of a mile north of the Inn, almost opposite the Ashop Clough path to Hayfield. It runs quite steeply up through thick forest at about 45 degrees across the hillside, emerging by a stile and signpost. The path continues up, but be careful not to go along the hillside on the line of the old Roman road. There is a rather indistinct junction. Pause on this section to look back at the superb views of Kinder—they can be

dramatic if the light is right—and up Ashop Clough. An excellent level shooters' path runs high up the hillside above the stream and just under the lip of the moor right round towards the headwaters. Walk a little way up the gully which turns north, cross it—and from then on it is rough walking with no path. The direction, however, is easy—due north. Keep east of the headwaters of Birchin Clough, otherwise you'll have some peat gully scrambling. You are heading for the almost straight gully running west to east (almost) from the headwaters of Nether Reddale. If you miss it, there is some very difficult ground—wet peat and groughs—but if you are on course, turn westerly along the channel into Nether Reddale Clough. From here the going improves a lot. A faint path leads down, on the lip, well above the steeply descending stream.

In effect, with minor variations, from now on you follow the lip of the moor, round into Upper Reddale Clough and on up the Alport. There are good long distance views over the hills to the Eastern Edges, and the views down to the waterfalls of the Alport are probably superior to those from the main path on the other side. A quarter of a mile before Grains-in-the-Water, the path (faint and intermittent) leaves the lip, and traverses across and down the hillside to the watersmeet.

This route up the Alport can also be reached from Birchin Clough, though the walk is inferior to that just described. If you decide to try it, don't go up the Clough which is thickly forested, but up the gap in the trees just north of the bridge, and on to the open moor. Take your pick then—it's all rough—either north until you hit the Alport, or north for about a mile and then east into the Reddale Cloughs. There is also a route to Grains-in-the-Water direct from the Snake Road up the Upper North Grain path, and then north, but I don't find it very rewarding, and you miss all the beauty of the Alport Valley.

# BLEAKLOW RIDGE
## Map 18

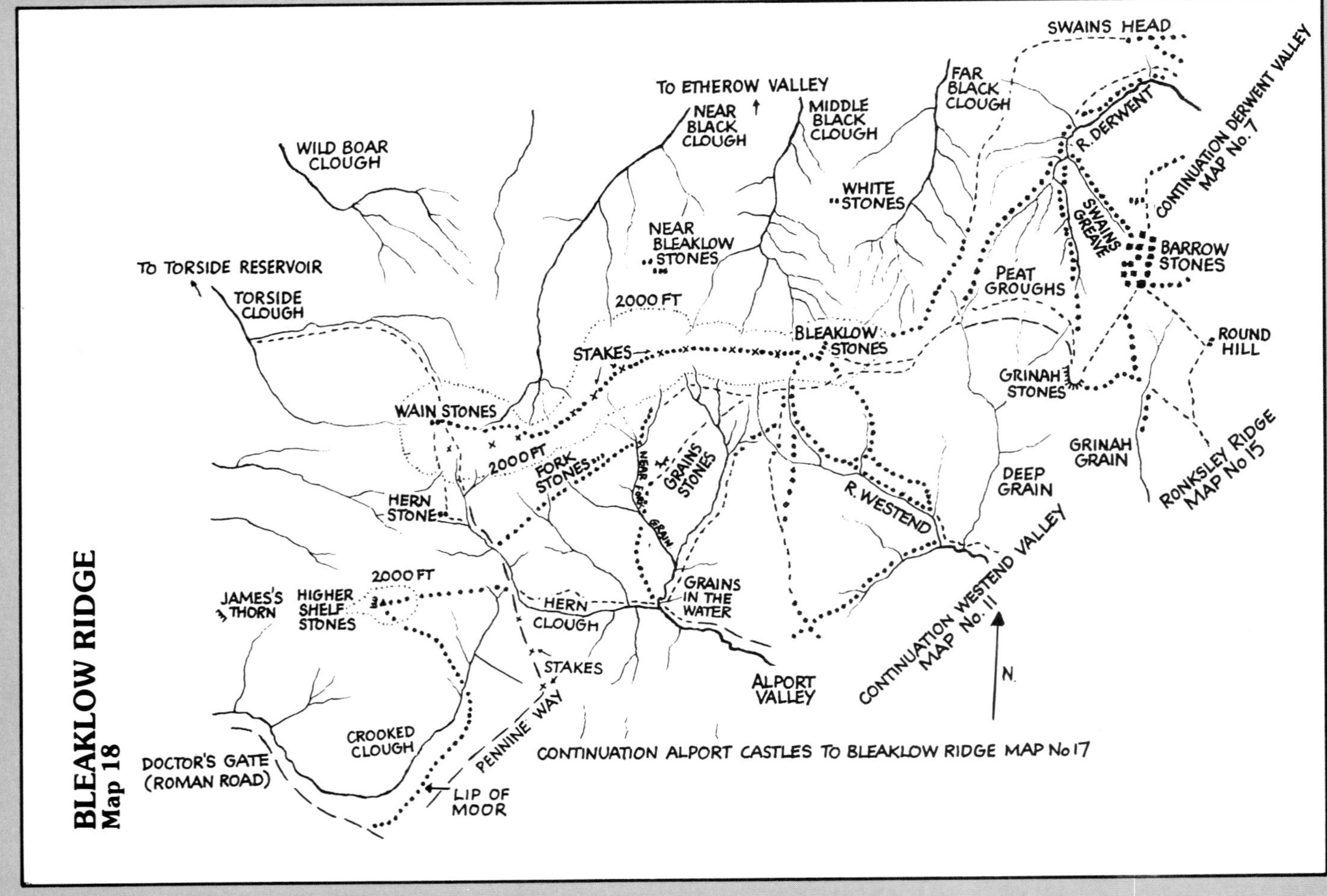

# CHAPTER 12

# THE TOPS

# BLEAKLOW RIDGE

# HIGHER SHELF, WAIN, BLEAKLOW, BARROW STONES

This is the highest part of the area covered by this study, much of it being above 2,000 feet. To the north, the ground falls away down heathery slopes to the east-west valley of the Etherow. To the south are the comparatively long valleys of the Alport and Westend, and in the east the Derwent. In my view the scenery is much more varied and attractive to the south than to the north, and the eastern end is generally superior to the west.

At the outset, let me mention the section of the Pennine Way from the Snake Pass via Hern Clough and  Wain Stones to Crowden. This long distance "Path" has been the subject of a number of guide books and I do not propose to add more than a few sentences to what has already been said more than adequately. The "Way" offers approaches to the Bleaklow Ridge from the north in the area of Torside Reservoir, and from the Snake Pass summit, but cannot, I think, be recommended. Almost the entire distance is a morass of

peat, churned up by thousands of boots and becoming worse year by year. The Peak National Park Authority has gallantly tried several methods of halting or reducing the erosion, but nothing so far has been really effective—I doubt whether there is a satisfactory solution. It is a great pity that the first and usually only glimpse of the Bleaklow area for thousands of walkers from other parts of the country should be from this path. It certainly gives a poor impression.

The easiest approach from the west, i.e. the Glossop area, is via Doctor's Gate, switching, as the old Roman(?) road flattens beyond Urchin Clough to a vague path on the southern lip of Crooked Clough. This can be followed, with pleasant views across the valley and back towards Glossop, for quite a long way until the clough climbs more steeply—just beyond the more pronounced waterfall. From there a turn north up the easy grassy hill-side leads to Higher Shelf Stones. It is also possible to go straight on into Hern Clough. Note this route can also be joined from the Snake Pass by cutting across the moor. The views from Higher Shelf Stones (and from James's Thorn) are excellent, especially to the south and west and are well worth the climb on a good day. The strange human desire for some immortality has led to a defacement of the rocks themselves. The engines of the Super Fortress, which plunged into the hillside just after the 1939-45 War, still lie in the peat just to the east of the Trig point. I can remember seeing this wreck more than thirty years ago, when the entire fuselage and tail reared out of the hillside. It was an awsome sight. Since then official agencies and, over the years, souvenir hunters have reduced it to the engines and a few other pieces—please note that it is illegal to do any digging or remove any pieces of wrecked aricraft without first obtaining the permission of the landowner and the Ministry of Defence.

# THE TOPS
## Bleaklow Ridge—Higher Shelf Stones to Barrow Stones

Although this book is concerned mainly with the Derwent watershed, I had better mention routes from the north.

Leaving to one side the Pennine Way route already mentioned, the best approaches are (a) from just west of Salters Brook bridge, via Far Small Clough to Swains Head, or (b) from Fiddler's Green via Round Hill into Hoar Clough Head. Further west, in the area of the three Black Cloughs, access is possible, but the climb is rather rough and long—and not very rewarding. Generally speaking all the routes form the Etherow Valley involve a steady, heathery climb and none of them is of a hill-walking quality.

Much better, if possible, to approach from the south, using the valleys of the Derwent, Westend or Alport or the ridges in between. (See appropriate chapters.)

I will deal with the main ridge from east to west—walkers coming the other way should have little trouble in reversing it.

Barrow Stones will repay a little quiet exploration. It is really a whole stratum of Millstone Grit exposed on the hilltop and subsequent weathering has carved and moulded the rocks into Henry Moore-like shapes. On a still afternoon, with a slight mist lying on the hills, it is a very strange place to be, and people with fear-producing imaginations should, perhaps, avoid it—especially when daylight is failing. Have a look at the Crow Stone—unmistakable, opposite Round Hill on the southern side. The views to the north towards Black Hill and Holme Moss The Mast is clearly visible) are quite good, but usually a bit sullen. The best views are on the other side of the stones, looking south. Artistically, the view is somewhat marred by the foreground being not a great deal lower, (see Grinah Stones—a very similar view but better) but it is very extensive. The heather is soft, and the rocks offer reasonable shelter so it is a good place for a leisurely half hour.

The best descents (or ascents) are as follows:

**(1) Due north from the stones on a faint path which fades out at the lower rocks. Then down the hillside north of Barrow Clough to the River Derwent, choosing the grassier, drier route.**

**(2) Across the heather to the head of Barrow Clough, and down the clough on the north side—there is a faint path in places.**

**(3) Directly from the Crown Stone down the hillside on a fairly clear path and across to Round Hill, then turn for Ronksley.**

**(4) Pick a way due south into the headwaters of Grinah Grain. This is the safest in mist.**

There is now a clear path from the Crown Stone along the contour (direction slightly south of south-west) to Grinah Stones. This is a huge and fascinating mass of rocks, jutting out due south in the form of a nose. Unlike Barrow, the rocks are not spread across the hillside, but are piled up facing west and south. It is also worth noting (especially in winter) that they provide excellent shelter, If you choose the right spot, no matter which way the wind is blowing. The view, looking south, is in my opinion unequalled in the area. The ground falls away steeply to Grinah Grain and the Westend Valley so that, in good visibility, the eye moves away down the Derwent Valley over half of Derbyshire. Note the tiny triangle of the Ladybower Reservoir near the Dam itself visible about eight miles away. You sometimes see the reflected flash of a car windsreen on the road alongside. The whole of the Eastern Edges to Stanage and beyond run down the east, Bamford Edge, and Win Hill are etched out beautifully, the hump of Lose Hill peeps out beyond and to the left of Crookstone, with the long level mass of the Kinder plateau stretching out to the west.

In extremely clear weather, Longstone
Edge and some of the hills round Matlock
can be identified—try it.

Grinah is a worthy objective for a day's walk,
and an hour spent lolling in the heather on a
warm summer's day is heavenly.

A clear path leaves Grinah, due north at
first, turning westerly, for Bleaklow Stones.
Actually there are two paths. The plainest
one, after crossing a deep gully (one of the
headwaters of Deep Grain) curves round
the hillside before dropping into another of
the Deep Grain gullies. A fainter path goes
round the head of the first gully, and then
on the lip of the moor, past two small
groups of rocks, before descending to the
same gully. From there on, the path is
somewhat erratic, but except in thick mist,
can be followed quite easily to Bleaklow
Stones, which stand out ahead clearly. The
Trident, a huge block in three parts, is
quite impressive.

Though somewhat higher than Barrow and
Grinah, the view (though extensive) is not
quite so good as that from either of the
others. Neither are the rocks themselves
anything like as impressive. However, it is
a high wild spot and certainly worth visiting.
Walkers interested in height will note that
at 2,060 feet, it is the highest point in the
Peak District apart from Kinder (though
Wain Stones are only marginally lower).

There is another route from Barrow to
Bleaklow Stones, somewhat more direct
and keeping to the higher ground (a line of
stakes lead up towards Bleaklow Stones—
marked on the 2½ inch map) but the
entire route involves a slog over peat
groughs and loose peat which is usually
pretty wet. So much effort is involved, that
there is no time or inclination to look at the
view even when there is one, and the
route via Grinah is infinitely superior.

Remember that along all this stretch from
Barrow, in deteriorating winter conditions, a
comparative haven can be fairly easily reached
by turning due south for the Westend Valley
(see the chapter on Navigation).



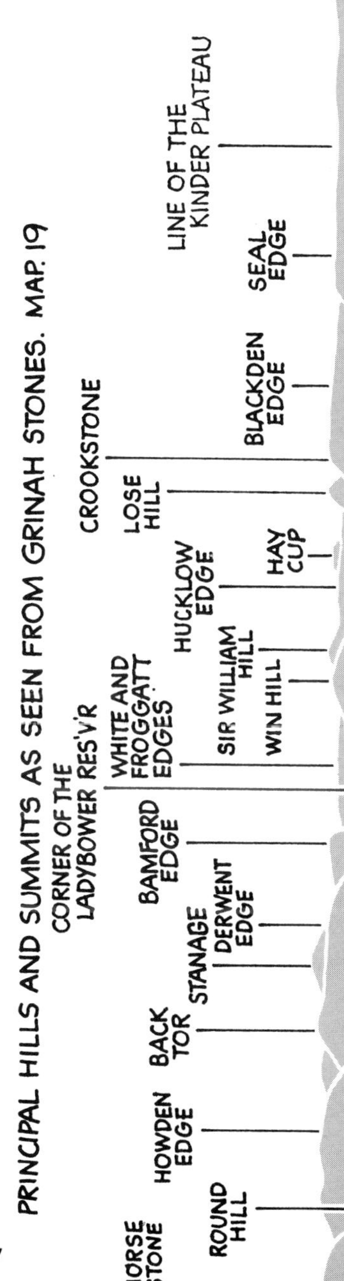

# THE TOPS
## Bleaklow Ridge – Higher Shelf Stones to Barrow Stones

The stretch from Bleaklow Stones to Wain Stones, though it doesn't look far on the map, requires a great expanse of energy. The pleasant, open area immediately to the west of Bleaklow Stones, soon gives way to peat groughs and these continue in varying sizes all the rest of the way (unless you hit one of the few more rocky areas). It is rather a punishing walk, with little to see, and you are likely to finish rather peaty round the lower legs. The line of stakes may be followed, but I always find it rather better, towards the end, to join one of the westward pointing headwaters of Near Black Clough. If you choose the right one, it will bring you out quite pleasantly just east of Wain Stones.

In my view, a better and much more rewarding walk is to keep to the south of the main ridge. The views are good almost all the way, and the going is much better. Move from Bleaklow Stones in a south-westerly direction, and after losing about 200 feet of height, you should pick up a vague path running east-west. It can be followed into the headwaters of the Alport. Do not continue up the main gullies (or you will be back among the groughs) but pick a way (no path) south-west over to the headwaters of Near Fork Grain. A group of prominent stones (walkers refer to them as Fork Stones, but they are not so named on the O.S. map) will be plainly seen along the hillside to the west, and you should pick up a path again in that direction. There is another fine view from these stones—and also a rough rock shelter, which though unwholesome, would be a life-saver in desperate conditions. The faint path disappears when the more peaty ground is reached, but continue somewhat south of west to Hern Clough. The going on this section is not very good, but a lot better than on the main ridge. From Hern Clough, you can turn north up the Pennine Way to Wain Stones, or wander on to Higher Shelf. Or, if you've had enough and the car is at the Westend forest gate, turn on a reasonable path running on the north side of Hern Clough pleasantly down to Grains-in-the-Water.

An interesting group of rocks to visit, and a good viewpoint, is Grain Stones. They are not named on the O.S. map, but jut out from the main ridge between Alport Head and Near Fork Grain. An approach can be made from Grains-in-the-Water or from further up the Alport, or by diverging from the east-west route described above, in the high headwaters of Near Fork Grain. The rocks are large and tumbled, and provide some convenient perches for contemplation.

# SUGGESTED WALKS

# CHAPTER 13

# SUGGESTED WALKS

Fairly brief details of the walks are given here as it is hoped that armchair pleasure will be obtained from working them out using the appropriate detailed maps to which reference is made.

Please note also that—as a study of the maps will show—all these walks can be shortened or lengthened according to taste (and ability).



1. Road to Ladybower Inn (cross road with care)—track beside pub to foot of Highshaw Clough, near Cut-Throat Bridge—abrupt turn west (left)—path to Whinstone Tor—north east on the Edge to the signposted Derwent-Moscar footpath—turn left (west) on this footpath via Grindle Barn to reservoir track—turn south on track back to the layby.

   **2/3 hours—Easy. Map No. 12 Chapter 6.**

2. Cross the viaduct—turn right on Derwent Road—turn left on farm track and bridleway via Crookhill Farm and Open Hagg to junction with Jaggers' route—turn right via Lockerbrook Farm (cut-off via path to Fairholmes possible here) to the foot of Ouzelden Clough—turn right on road back to Derwent Dam—road (little traffic) then track on east side of reservoir back to layby.

   **3/4 hours—Easy. Map Nos. 12 and 16 Chapters 1 and 9.**

3. Road to Ladybower Inn—track for 50 yards then path at rear of Ladybower Inn—steep climb up the hillside via Lead Hill and Whinstone Tor to Derwent Edge—along edge via White Tor and Dovestone Tor to Back Tor—northwest to Lost Lad and Hillend (cut-off possible here back to Derwent via Mill Brook)—path Abbey Bank to bottom of Abbey Brook—reservoir track back to layby.

   **5/6 hours—Generally easy—some rougher going on the edge. Map Nos. 12 and 9 Chapters 6 and 2.**

# FROM FAIRHOLMES PICNIC SITE

There are several short (½ hour) walks in the well signposted area around the dam and through the woods to the west, including a steep ascent through the forest to Lockerbrook farm—path just opposite the exit from the picnic site. A free leaflet gives details—ask at the Information Point or take one from the dispenser at Fairholmes.

A pleasant time can also be spent in taking the path round the east end of the dam wall, and walking north along the reservoir—turning when you feel inclined. Map No. 6.

4.  Concessionary *(a note on concessionary paths; they are not public rights of way, and can be closed by the landowner in an emergency e.g. during fire risk, or if works are being carried out on or adjacent to the path, e.g. Forestry or Water Authority work)* path between road and reservoir to Bridge End—bridle path through forest to Open Hagg—turn right—bridle path via Lockerbrook Farm to the bottom of Ouzelden Clough—road back to Fairholmes.

    **1/2 hours—very easy. Map No. 16 Chapters 1 and 9.**

5.  As No. 4 to Open Hagg—concessionary path to open country—up ridge via Rowlee Pasture to Alport Castles—turn right on good path to Westend forest gate—a fairly long road walk back, unless the minibus service is operating.

    **3/4 hours—easy but usually wet over Rowlee Pasture. Map Nos. 16 and 5 Chapters 1 and 9.**

6.  Road below the dam south east to Mill Brook—continue on reservoir track for short distance—signposted path up the hillside via Grindle Barn to southern end of Derwent Edge—north via Dovestone Tor to Back Tor—north-west to Lost Lad, Hillend—path via Abbey Bank to bottom of Abbey Brook—reservoir track back to Fairholmes.

    **4/5 hours—generally easy—some rougher going on the Edges. Map Nos. 6, 12 and 9 Chapters 1 and 6.**

7.  Reservoir track north to bottom of Abbey Brook—Abbey Bank path to Hillend—Lost Lad—Back Tor—north east for a mile—turn west into the upper reaches of Abbey Brook—path on east side of gorge (quite spectacular) round to the ruined cabins—path down Abbey Brook to reservoir track.

    **4/5 hours—mostly easy but some rough going beyond Back Tor. Map Nos. 6, 9 and 10 Chapters 2 and 6.**

8.  Reservoir track north to bottom of Abbey Brook—Footpath up the valley to ruined cabins—cross Abbey Brook (can be difficult after heavy rain)—High Stones on Howden Edge via Wet Stones—Edge via Margery Hill to Cut Gate path—turn south west on path to Slippery Stones—reservoir track (east side) back.

    **5/6 hours—generally easy—some rougher going on the Edges. Map Nos. 6, 9, 10 and 13 Chapters 2 and 7.**

## FROM WESTEND FOREST GATE

9. Two "out and return" walks—one up
the valley track as far as say Grinah
Grain and the other up to Alport Castles
and a short way along the ridge.

   **1/2 hours—easy. Map No. 11
   Chapter 4.**

10. Path to Alport Castles—north west to
Trig Point—The Ridge—Bleaklow
Stones—Grinah Stones—Ronksley
Moor—track down Westend Valley.
(Note: can be extended to Barrow
Stones or shortened from Bleaklow
Stones direct into the Westend Valley).

    **5/6 hours—mostly rough going on
    the ridges and wild country
    (compass essential). Map Nos. 17,
    18 and 11 Chapters 4, 10 and 12.**

11. Track up the valley—path by the river
to headwaters of the Westend—
Bleaklow Ridge—Wain Stones—Hern
Clough—Grains-in-the-Water—Alport
Valley path then ridge to Alport
Castles—path back to gate. (Note: can
be extended via Higher Shelf Stones or
shortened by cutting out Wain Stones
and walking from Alport Head to
Grains-in-the-Water).

    **6/7 hours—rough going on the top
    sections and wild country (again
    compass essential). Map Nos. 11,
    18 and 17 Chapters 4, 12 and 11.**

## FROM THE KING'S TREE

There is always the gentle walk along the
track through the forest to the packhorse
bridge and Slippery Stones and then a little
way up the valley track—return the same
way.

**Map Nos. 7 and 8 Chapter 1.**

12. Track to Slippery Stones—Cut Gate
Path almost to the top—along the
hillside to Bull Stones (can be extended
to Rocking Stone)—down Broad Head
Clough to track and return.

    **2/3 hours—rough going on the
    Edge—otherwise easy. Map Nos.
    7, 8 and 13 Chapters 1, 2 and 7.**

13. Track to Slippery Stones—Cut Gate
path (or Bull Clough) Bull Stones—
Crow Stones—head of Stainery
Clough round to Horse Stone—edges
to Shepherds' Meeting Stones—Dean
Head—return down the valley path
then track. (Note: can be greatly
extended via Derwent Headwaters and
Barrow Stones, or shortened anywhere
by turning into the valley).

    **5/6 hours—rough going on the
    Edges—but walk back easy. Map
    Nos. 7, 8, and 13 Chapters 1, 2
    and 7.**

14. Turn left off track just over Linch
Clough stepping stones—Linch
Clough—Ronksley—Grinah Stones—
along to Barrow Stones—north west
into the headwaters of the Derwent—
return down the valley. (Note: can be
extended by continuing round
watershed via Dean Head and
Shepherds' Meeting Stones, or
shortened by walking direct into the
Derwent Valley from Barrow Stones).

    **5/6 hours—some rough going on
    the tops, but valley section easy.
    Compass essential. Map Nos. 7,
    15 and 18 Chapters 1, 3, 8 and 12.**

## FROM SNAKE INN

15. Path up Oyster Clough—north to Alport Valley—edge of valley to Grains-in-the-water—Hearn Clough—Wain Stones—south to Higher Shelf Stones—southern lip of Crooked Clough—Doctor's Gate—Snake Road—forestry concessionary path down Lady Clough.

**5/6 hours—a lot of rough going (allow time) and a compass essential. Map Nos. 17 and 18 Chapters 10, 11 and 12.**

May I point out again that all these routes are open to an almost infinite number of variations—different routes up—adding bits on and so on. The really tough guys can always walk round the entire watershed.

The following suggestions are, of course, my own personal views, but I think they are likely to meet with general agreement.

## BEST PLACES FOR DISTANT VIEWS

1. Lost Lad (Derwent Edge).
2. Rocking-Crow Stones (Eastern Edges) See Map No. 14 for skyline view.
3. Grinah Stones (Bleaklow Ridge).
4. Grains Stones (Bleaklow Ridge).
5. Higher Shelf Stones.

## BEST DESCENTS

1. Nose of Derwent Edge—Whinstone Tor to Ashopton.
2. Lost Lad—Abbey Bank—Abbey Brook.
3. Howden Edge (High Stones) to ruined cabins Abbey Brook.
4. Crow Stones—Broadhead Clough—valley.
5. Alport Castles—Westend Valley.
6. Oyster Clough—Snake Road.

## BEST PLACES FOR SILENT SOLITUDE

1. Upper waterfall—Stainery Clough.
2. Shepherds' Meeting Stones.
3. Westend Valley—watersmeet just north of Deep Grain.
4. Grains-in-the-Water.
5. Waterfalls in Grinah Grain.

*Ashopton Viaduct from Crook Hill*

# INDEX


## A

**Abbey Bank** 35, 42, 62, 65
**Abbey Brook** 32, 34, 35, 40, 42, 44, 63, 67
**Alport Castles** 32, 56, 60, 75, 77
**Alport Castles Farm** 77, 81
**Alport Head** 82, 88
**Alport Valley** 40, 55, 58, 62, 75, 77, 81, 83, 85, 86
**Ashopton** 28, 32, 34, 63, 75
**Ashop Valley** 76, 83

## B

**Back Tor** 32, 35, 41, 44, 63, 65
**Bamford Edge** 86
**Barrow Clough** 38, 53, 86
**Barrow Stones** 38, 51, 53, 57, 68, 71, 72, 85, 86, 87
**Berristers Tor** 42
**Birchen Clough** 83
**Birchinlee** 32, 42, 60
**Black Clough (Westend)** 57, 60, 78
**Black Clough (Bleaklow Ridge)** 38, 86, 88
**Black Hill** 86
**Blacklow Court** 57
**Bleaklow Ridge** 56, 59, 62, 67, 69, 78, 82, 85
**Bleaklow Stones** 38, 55, 58, 62, 71, 78, 82, 85, 87, 88
**Bradfield** 44
**Broadhead Clough** 36, 49, 69, 70
**Bull Clough** 40, 47, 48, 68
**Bull Stones** 48, 67, 68

## C

**Cakes o' Bread** 65
**Cogman Clough** 42
**Coldwell Clough** 38, 48, 70
**Coldwell Spring** 70
**Cowms Rocks** 83
**Cranberry Clough** 36, 40, 47, 49, 67
**Crooked Clough** 85
**Crook Hill** 75
**Crowden** 85
**Crown Stone** 53, 72, 86
**Crow Stones** 48, 49, 67, 68
**Cut Gate** 36, 47, 48, 62, 67, 68
**Cutthroat Bridge** 65

## D

**Dean Head Stones** 68
**Deep Grain** 39, 55, 58, 59, 87
**Deer Holes** 52
**Derwent Edge** 28, 34, 63, 65, 75
**Derwent Reservoir** 32, 35, 51, 69
**Derwent Source** 38, 68
**Derwent Valley** 28, 36, 40, 48, 49, 53, 67, 68, 71, 85, 86
**Derwent Village** 28, 34
**Ditch Clough** 56, 60
**Doctor's Gate** 85
**Dovestone Tor** 32, 65
**Dry Clough** 57
**Duke's Road** 44

## E

**Etherow Valley** 38, 86

## F

**Fagney Clough** 56, 60
**Fairholmes** 28, 32, 34, 36
**Fiddler's Green** 38, 48, 68, 86
**Flouch Inn** 62, 67
**Foul Clough** 46

## G

**Glethering Clough** 78
**Glossop** 85
**Grainfoot** 18, 34
**Grains-in-the-Water** 62, 81, 82, 88
**Grains Stones** 82, 88
**Gravy Clough** 42
**Green Clough** 60
**Grinah Grain** 55, 57, 58, 72, 86
**Grinah Stones** 38, 39, 51, 53, 56, 57, 62, 71, 72, 86, 87

## H

**Hagg Farm** 75
**Hagg Side** 34
**Heardman, Fred** 39
**Hern Clough** 82, 85, 88
**Higher Shelf Stones** 82, 85, 88
**High Stones** 46, 67
**Hillsend** 65
**Hobson Moor Dike** 41
**Hoar Clough** 38, 40, 48, 53, 68, 70, 86
**Hoar Stones** 48, 68,
**Hollin Clough** 35
**Holme Moss** 69, 86
**Horse Stone** 53, 67, 68, 70
**Horse Stone Naze** 70
**Horse Stone Spring** 48, 70
**Howden Clough** 34, 35, 46, 67
**Howden Edge** 35, 40, 41, 44, 46, 67
**Howden House** 46, 55
**Howden Reservoir** 32, 35, 55, 69, 75
**Howshaw Tor** 44
**Humber Knoll** 38
**Hurst Clough** 32

## J

**Jagger's Route** 34, 65
**James's Thorn** 85

## K

**Kinder Scout** 56, 62, 67, 69, 71, 76, 77, 83, 86, 87
**King's Tree** 28, 32, 36, 51, 71

## L

**Ladybower Inn** 65
**Ladybower Reservoir** 28, 65, 86
**Lady Clough** 79
**Lands Clough** 38
**Langsett** 48
**Lead Hill** 32
**Linch Clough** 32, 36, 40, 51, 72
**Lockerbrook Farm** 75
**Long Edge** 47
**Longstone Edge** 87
**Lose Hill** 71, 86
**Lost Lad** 32, 35, 42, 65
**Lower Small Clough** 52, 57, 71
**Loxley** 41

## M

**Margery Hill** 47, 67
**Matlock** 87
**Mill Brook** 32
**Miry Clough** 78, 81
**Moscar** 34, 62, 65

## N

**Near Fork Grain** 88
**Nether Reddale Clough** 40, 81, 83

## O

**Outer Edge** 38, 48, 68
**Ouzelden Clough** 32, 51, 60, 75
**Oyster Clough** 83

## P

**Packhorse Bridge** 34, 36
**Penistone Stile** 46
**Pennine Way** 62, 82, 85, 88

## R

**Ravens Clough** 58, 59, 60, 78
**Ridge Clough** 59, 71
**Ridgewalk Moor** 57
**Robin Hood's Spring** 46
**Rocking Stone** 69
**Roman Road** 83, 85
**Ronksley Moor** 51, 52, 55, 57, 71, 86
**Round Hill** 53, 71, 86
**Rowlee Pasture** 76, 77

## S

**Salter's Brook** 38, 86
**Sheepfold Clough** 41, 44, 65
**Shepherd's Meeting Stones** 68
**Slippery Stones** 34, 35, 36, 48, 62, 67
**Snake Inn** 81, 83
**Snake Road** 75, 77, 81, 83, 85
**Stainery Clough** 36, 40, 48, 62, 68, 69, 70
**Stanage Edge** 86
**Strines** 44, 62, 65

## T

**Torside Reservoir** 85

## U

**Upper North Grain** 83
**Upper Small Clough** 36, 53
**Urchin Clough** 85

## W

**Wain Stones** 62, 82, 85, 88
**Wet Stones** 46
**Westend Farm** 56, 60
**Westend Head** 55, 71, 77
**Westend Valley** 40, 55, 56, 58, 59, 60, 71, 75, 77, 85, 86, 87
**Wheel Stones** 32, 65
**Whinstone Lee Tor** 65
**White Tor** 32
**Win Hill** 65, 71, 86